MW00436218

THE
WHOLE
STORY
for the whole
family
A YEAR OF
JESUS-CENTERED FAMILY
devotions

Michael Kelley

THE WHOLE STORY

for the whole family

A YEAR OF

JESUS-CENTERED FAMILY devotions

B&H
PUBLISHING
NASHVILLE, TENNESSEE

Published by B&H Publishing Group
Nashville, Tennessee

Dewey Decimal Classification: 242.2
Subject Heading: DEVOTIONAL LITERATURE / BIBLE—
STUDY AND TEACHING / JESUS CHRIST

Cover design by B&H Publishing Group.
Author photo by Randy Hughes.

1 2 3 4 5 6 • 25 24 23 22 21

To Joshua, Andi, and Christian

This book really came from you guys.
Thank you for showing up for breakfast on time.

Acknowledgments

I remain so thankful for a partner in ministry at Broadman & Holman Publishing. Thank you, Devin Maddox and Taylor Combs, for helping me flesh out this idea, polishing out a scope and sequence, and then ultimately reading through a ton of object lessons. It means the world to me that you continue to believe in me as a writer and as a friend.

I also am indebted to so many families with whom we have had the joy to walk in this parenting journey. We are all different, and yet we are all the same. I have learned so much from you in what it means to be a dad and to invest in all aspects of the lives of our children.

I would also like to acknowledge the fact that the work on this book took place primarily in 2020, the year when our churches were physically closed for a significant period of time. As such, parents all over the world have had to take a greater degree of initiative to try and help their children read, know, and understand God's Word. These have been difficult days, but even the most difficult days are to be redeemed. And by God's grace, perhaps one of the ways this time will be redeemed is that moms and dads everywhere will continue that pattern of spiritual investment.

Introduction

Deuteronomy 6 contains the text of the *shema*. That word literally means "hear," and it's the beginning of the greatest command:

> "Hear, O Israel: The LORD our God, the LORD is one. Love the LORD your God with all your heart, with all your soul and with all your strength." (Deut. 6:4–5 NIV)

This is the oldest fixed prayer in Judaism, and even today is recited at least twice a day by observant Jews. This is also the answer that Jesus gave when an expert in the law asked Him what the greatest command was:

> "Love the Lord your God with all your heart, with all your soul, and with all your mind. This is the greatest and most important command." (Matt. 22:37–38)

This—loving God with all of our being—frames everything else. In fact, you might rightly say that if we get this right, everything else will fall into place because the love of God forms the framework for every other action, attitude, and decision we make. The text in Deuteronomy goes on to emphasize just how important this is, and it's in this emphasis that we also find a command for us as parents:

"These words that I am giving you today are to be in your heart. Repeat them to your children. Talk about them when you sit in your house and when you walk along the road, when you lie down and when you get up. Bind them as a sign on your hand and let them be a symbol on your forehead. Write them on the doorposts of your house and on your city gates." (Deut. 6:6–9)

There is no doubt that we, as parents, should be the primary spiritual influence on our children. This responsibility cannot—and should not—be delegated to a church program, though we should work in concert with the church for the overall growth of our kids in Christ. One of the simplest ways we do that is through a devoted, regular, set-aside time to read and study the Bible together.

I've known that to be true, and yet I haven't always been a family devotion guy.

It's not because I didn't want or aspire to be; I did. But we went a long time as a family before pulling the trigger and trying to integrate this practice into the regular rhythm of our family life.

There are a lot of reasons, I think, for my delay. Part of it was convenience; I wasn't ready to alter our schedule to accommodate that fifteen or twenty minutes. Part of it was nervousness; I wasn't sure if I could do this well. But the biggest part of the reason for my procrastination was really about having a clear direction to get started.

By God's grace, we've been doing morning devotions together for almost ten years now—long enough for this practice to be ingrained in our regular routine. It's a long road, as are most things, especially with young children. Though revival doesn't break out every morning over eggs and toast, our continued hope and prayer is that times like these build into the love and discipline our children will have in the future when it comes to God's Word.

The goal of this resource, then, is to put forth that simple, clear direction for other parents who, like me, find themselves struggling to get started or to remain consistent. Each daily devotion is meant to be simple and achievable, with five components:

> **Show:** Each day begins with a simple object lesson or game designed to introduce the text. It's an easy way to capture attention and generate conversation.
>
> **Read:** Then there is a specific text of Scripture given. These texts are organized chronologically so kids can see that though there are many stories in the Bible, it's really just one big story that has Jesus as the main character.
>
> **Explain:** Next comes a brief explanation of the text. This is meant to help a parent not just read the text with their children, but then offer a little background and easy-to-understand commentary to help kids see not only what the text means, but where it fits in the overall story of the Bible.
>
> **Reflect:** There are three reflection questions each day that are easy to answer, and will hopefully solidify the story for the kids and also help them see how that text applies to their daily lives.
>
> **Pray:** Finally, there is a brief prayer to close out the devotion.

You'll also notice that there are only four devotions per week. This is intentional so that on Friday, or another day of the week, you can take a brief break and spend your devotion time praying for one another and expressing gratitude for what God is doing in and through you.

Simple, repeatable, and achievable. And, by God's grace, also foundational—not only foundational in providing a good sketch of the Bible for kids, but foundational in pushing down the daily habit of getting in God's Word and being nourished by it. Going back to Deuteronomy 6:

> "These words that I am giving you today are to be in your heart. Repeat them to your children. Talk about them when you sit in your house and when you walk along the road, when you lie down and when you get up. Bind them as a sign on your hand and let them be a symbol on your forehead. Write them on the doorposts of your house and on your city gates." (Deut. 6:6–9)

Repeat the Word of God. Talk about His commands when you're coming and going, when you wake up and when you go to bed. They should be as ready in our minds as if we had them written on our hands and foreheads. In other words, talk of God and His Word should be the constant backdrop to every conversation.

But before you get started, can I share with you one warning about this pattern of family devotion?

The potential impact and power of that family devotion will no doubt be minimized if the *only* time you talk about the things of God is in that single environment.

If the only time our family prays, or talks about Jesus, or points each other to the truth of God is during that fifteen minutes, then we are subtly emphasizing to our kids that the Bible is for spiritual times. But the rest of the day, we just have to live our lives. This is not a Deuteronomy 6 kind of devotion. In fact, if we do this, we are treating the family devotion time like a magic formula—something we check off on our list as parents that we think will ensure our kids will love and follow Jesus.

Don't think of your family devotion as the destination; think of it as the launching pad for all the other moments you have during the day. Come back to the Word again and again. That doesn't mean you have to have multiple, set-aside times for the reading and study of God's Word. That, too, seems to violate the spirit of Deuteronomy 6.

Instead, you want to have a family culture that is rooted in God's Word so that it indeed is the constant background of everything else you do. You want it to be the most natural thing in the world when a child is discouraged, or when a family decision has to be made, or when you are simply processing what's happening in the world together to bring up what God says about this situation in His book.

Yes, parents, read the Bible together. Yes, parents, set aside a time to do so. But also move toward not just a moment, but a "when you" kind of philosophy so that the Word of God might be deeply rooted in the minds and hearts of your family.

Everything from Nothing

Show

Distribute pen and paper, Legos, Play-Dough, or some other material to each family member. Explain that they will have two minutes to create something brand-new. It could be a new building, a new animal, a new food—anything new. Start the timer and allow the family to work. Once the work is done, allow each family member to explain what they made, commending each one for their creativity. Then explain that even though you all created new kinds of things, you all used materials to create them. You didn't create the Legos, the paper, or the Play-Dough. Even though you made something, you didn't make something from nothing. But that's what God did when He created.

Read

Genesis 1:1–5

Explain

The Bible tells us that in the beginning, there was God, and God alone. He has always been, and He will always be. When He created, God didn't use material that was already present; instead, He created all things just by speaking them into existence. Everywhere we look we can see evidences of God's power, His creativity, and His love. There is no one and nothing like God who has the power to bring things into existence by His power. Every time we see a tree, a cloud, or a mountain, it's a chance to remember the powerful God who spoke it all into existence. As the story continues, we will see that we need a powerful God to do what we could never do for ourselves.

Reflect

1. What does God's creation show us about Him?

2. How should we respond to a God so powerful that He can create something from nothing?

3. What are some of your favorite things in the world that remind you of how powerful God is?

Pray

Thank You, God, that You are powerful. Help us today, as we walk through the world You made, to remember that You are the Creator of all things.

In His Image

Show

If you have them, gather together some family photo albums and spend a few minutes comparing the way different relatives tend to resemble each other. Compare fathers and mothers to sons and daughters, or go back several generations if possible. But beyond that, also point out that children often adopt the same mannerisms and sayings as their parents. Point out a few examples of this in your own home if you can. Then explain that children take on the characteristics of their parents. In a similar way, when God created human beings, He made them in a special and unique way. God made men and women in His image.

Read

Genesis 1:26–31

Explain

God created everything from nothing, but the way He created people was completely unique. Unlike the stars, the mountains, or the animals, God created men and women in His image. That means human beings share some characteristics with God. For example, we can love God and each other in a way that plants and animals never could. We are meant to have a real relationship with the God of the universe—to love Him and love being with Him.

Because we are created in God's image, God also wants us to bring honor to Him in the way that we relate to the rest of His creation. We are to think, love, and act in the way God does. This is how we are meant to live, but as we'll soon find out, something happened that broke our ability to love this God who loves us so much.

Reflect

1. If every person is created in God's image, then how should we treat every person no matter who they are?

2. What are some ways we can all show we are created in God's image today?

3. Have you ever seen a person being treated like they weren't made in God's image?

Pray

Thank You, God, for making us in Your image. Help us to remember that our purpose is to love and glorify You in our lives.

A Day to Rest

Show

Explain to the family that you are going to play a game called "Quiet Statues." Whisper a kind of statue to each member of the family (snake, king, elephant, singer, etc.). At the count of three, every family member has to freeze into their statue, and remain in that position until someone moves. The person who moves first tries to identify what kind of statue each person is making. Explain that sometimes we think resting just means being still and quiet. But chances are, when they were making their statues, they didn't feel much like resting. Explain further that God wants us to rest, but to God, resting means something more than just being still and quiet.

Read

Genesis 2:1–3

Explain

After God made everything, He rested on the seventh day. But God didn't rest because He was tired from all His work; He rested because He was finished. He made everything He intended to make, in just the way He intended to make it. Everything was absolutely good in every way, so God rested because there was nothing left to do.

God also intends that we regularly rest, but resting for us is more than just taking a nap or being quiet. Resting for us means celebrating that God does everything in just the right way and at just the right time. When we rest each week, we are remembering that God always does what He intends to do. But while everything was perfect, a new character was about to enter the story. And what was perfect was about to be undone.

Reflect

1. What are some ways we can practice this kind of rest in our home, remembering who God is and what He has done?

2. Why is it sometimes hard for us to really take a break and rest?

3. What are some of the decisions we need to make in our home in order to make sure we are resting in the right way?

Pray

Thank You, God, that You do all things well. Help us to make choices that enable our family to rest in celebration of who You are and what You have done.

Hiding from God

Show

Gather the family, then ask them to play a game of "Speed Hide and Seek." Explain they will only have ten seconds to hide, and then go and find them. Explain that there were two reasons why it was so easy to find them—one is because they didn't have much time to hide; the other reason is because you know the house better than they do and knew where to immediately look. Explain that in today's part of the story, you will see together that the man and the woman hid from God, but it was not part of a game. It was because of something much more serious.

Read

Genesis 3:1–10

Explain

Everything was good in God's creation, but the man and the woman were deceived by the serpent. Instead of trusting that God is good and loving, they believed the serpent's lie that God was holding something back from them—that if He really loved them, He would have allowed them to eat from every single tree.

God's children believed these lies about Him, and they chose to disobey God. This disobedience is called sin. When the man and woman chose to sin, everything was broken in God's perfect universe, starting with their own reason for being. God had made His people to live lovingly with Him, but when they sinned, they began to hide from God. Their relationship was broken. And today, our relationship with God is still broken. We still disobey God's commands when we don't believe He gives them to us for our own good, and we still hide from the truth when we sin. We still live in this desperate situation, hiding from our Father, and we will continue to do so unless God comes and finds us.

Reflect

1. Why did the man and the woman choose to disobey God even though He had done so much for them?

2. Why do you think sin makes people hide from God?

3. Why is it foolish to hide from God?

Pray

God, we are all sinners. Help us to remember how foolish it is to hide from You, and help us to trust You even when we have been disobedient.

A Promise in the Darkness

Show

Put a cookie or a small piece of chocolate before the family, and ask for a volunteer to eat it. Then take a few dashes of Tabasco sauce and put it on top of the treat, and ask the same question. If someone is willing to eat it, ask the person how the addition changed the treat. Explain that even though it might seem like just a little something was added, the "something" changed the whole treat. Further explain that sometimes something very small can have a huge effect, even bigger than we realize. This is just a small illustration of what happened when Adam and Eve chose to sin.

Read

Genesis 3:11–24

Explain

Actions have consequences. Adam and Eve's choice to believe the lies instead of the truth about God had consequences we still feel today. Everything was broken in God's perfect world. Humans were hiding, their work would become harder, and they would not be able to carry out their purpose in the world. Not only that, but all of creation was turned upside down.

In fact, everywhere in the world today where we see evil, destruction, and pain is a result of the brokenness of God's creation. Darkness has entered the story, but even in the midst of darkness, God shone the light of a promise. He promised that one day, Someone would come who would put an end to darkness and evil. This Someone, Jesus, would defeat the serpent and his schemes and everything that had been broken would be put right again. The only way we can come out from hiding and start to see things put right again is through Jesus.

Reflect

1. What are some examples of the brokenness of God's creation you see in the world around you?

2. What promise did God make in the midst of the darkness?

3. Why is it important that we believe in Jesus?

Pray

We're sorry, God, that we still sin. Help us to trust in Your promise even when things seem dark in the world around us.

Brother against Brother

Show

Gather a clear glass of water and some food coloring. Display the glass in front of the family and ask them what they see. Of course, the water is clear and clean. Then put one drop of food coloring in it and watch how the food coloring moves throughout the water, eventually coloring every part. Explain that in our story, Adam and Eve sinned, and from that one single act everything since then has been colored with sin. As the story continues today, we will see how dramatically things changed just after Adam and Eve left the garden.

Read

Genesis 4:1–8

Explain

Remember that when God made Adam and Eve, part of His commands to them were to have children together and fill the earth. Adam and Eve were obeying this command of God, and they had two sons together named Cain and Abel. But even their attempts to obey God was colored by sin, and the two boys found themselves in conflict with one another.

The boys, like their parents, knew they were made to honor and worship God. Abel brought a sacrifice to God that represented

17

his very best—the best sheep of his flock. But Cain did not, and he was jealous and angry with his brother. He was so angry that he killed him. This is the first murder in the history of the world, and it was because everything is colored by sin.

So also today all our hearts are colored with sin. We cannot escape it. Even when we try to do the right thing, we often do so for the wrong reason because our hearts, like everything else, are broken and affected by sin. And yet even in our sin, God is merciful to us. We can only come to Him by His grace, and as we will see, He is always ready to receive us.

Reflect

1. What was the difference between Cain and Abel's sacrifice?

2. Why did the Lord accept Abel's sacrifice but not Cain's?

3. We don't bring animals to sacrifice to God today, but what are some ways that we give God our best to honor and worship Him?

Pray

God, we know that our hearts are colored with sin. Help us to see the sin in ourselves, and help us not to hide from it, but instead to quickly confess it to You.

Judgment and Rescue

Show

Place several objects on the ground so that it would be difficult to walk straight through them without stepping on one. Then blindfold one family member, and explain that you are going to guide them through the objects using only voice commands. Try the experiment, then ask the family to consider what would have to be true in order for a person to make it through the obstacles without stepping on one. Point out that two things must be true—the person giving directions must be clear and trustworthy, and the person following directions must be trusting and obedient. If you gave faulty instructions, or if the person listening did not trust your instructions were true, then he or she would inevitably not make it through. Explain that as the story continues today, we will meet a man who had his own set of obstacles. He demonstrated his faith in God by listening to God's commands and doing exactly what He said.

Read

Genesis 6:11–22

Explain

By the time of Noah, sin had spread so much and so deeply through the world that God had had enough. He decided to judge the whole earth for sin, wiping everything away and starting all over again. This is the true judgment for sin—it is so serious that the only just judgment is death. But even in God's judgment, He provided a way of rescue and escape. He spoke to a man named Noah, one person who found favor in God's eyes. Noah, the Bible tells us, was the lone righteous man in his generation. He walked with God, and God considered him righteous not because he was without sin, but instead because of his faith. And how do we know that Noah's faith was real? It's simply because he believed God when God told him He was going to destroy the earth, and he showed that obedience by building the ark. This ark became the vessel of rescue, the one way Noah, his family, and the animals could escape judgment.

The same penalty for sin exists today. Sin is as serious as it's ever been, and the penalty is death. But as with Noah, God has provided a way of escape if we will believe in Him. Noah escaped judgment through the ark; we escape judgment through faith in Jesus.

Reflect

1. Why do we need to be rescued, just like Noah did?

2. In what ways is the ark like Jesus?

3. How do we know if we truly believe in God like Noah did?

Pray

Lord, we know that sin is serious, and that the judgment for sin is death. Thank You for providing a way that we can be rescued from judgment through Jesus.

Never Again

Show

Place a piece of white paper on a table or on the floor in the sunlight coming in from the window. Then, fill a clear glass about half full of water. Slowly place the glass on the white paper in the sunlight, and a rainbow should appear as the sunlight shines through the glass and onto the paper. If the rainbow doesn't appear, you may need to lift the glass slightly, or tip it to an angle in order to make the rainbow display on the paper. Explain to the family that in today's part of the story, we will see the very first rainbow, and understand what it means.

Read

Genesis 9:1–16

Explain

Noah, his family, and the animals had been in the ark for almost a year. After forty days and nights of rain, the water slowly began to recede, and eventually it was time for everyone to come out of the ark. As they came out, Noah offered a sacrifice of worship to God, and God made a promise to Noah. This kind of promise God made is called a covenant, and in this covenant, God promised He would never again destroy the earth with a flood. As a sign of His promise, God put the rainbow in the sky.

Sadly, while God had wiped the earth clean, the sin that was in the world was still in the hearts of His people. And though God would not destroy the earth by flood ever again, He would still bring about judgment for the sin that was still in the world. But the rainbow reminds us that though God will judge, He is merciful; He has promised that we have a way to be rescued from our sin and the judgment that is still to come. Today, we can still look to the rainbow that comes after the rain and remember not only God's promise to Noah, but also that God keeps all His promises to us.

Reflect

1. What does it mean when we see a rainbow in the sky?

2. How can we be rescued from God's judgment of our sin?

3. How should we respond when we see God's rainbow after the rain?

Pray

Thank You, God, that You are just. And thank You that even in Your justice You provide a way of rescue for those who trust in You.

Pride in Our Hearts

Show

Prior to devotion, gather an assortment of regular household items (a cereal box, a pencil, a book, etc.). There should be a pretty wide variety of materials (at least ten) for the activity. Tell the family that they are to use the materials provided to build a tower as high as they can. Give them a couple of chances to build the tower until they think it's as high as it can possibly go. If the tower falls, all the better. Explain that as the story continues today, you will see a group of people who thought they, too, could build a tower—one so high it could reach to heaven.

Read

Genesis 11:1–9

Explain

Several generations passed after Noah came out of the ark, and once again the earth was filled with sin, because sin is not just something we do; it's inside of us, deep within our hearts. Back in the garden, Satan tempted Adam and Eve to reach beyond their purpose; he told them that they should not be content to be created in God's image, but instead should want to be gods themselves. In the same way, pride was so deep inside the hearts of the people that they wanted to be like God. They wanted to build a tower for their own glory. Instead of honoring and glorifying their Creator, they wanted to take His place.

God saw the pride of mankind and judged them once again, scattering them throughout the earth. Before, they all spoke the same language; but now they would have different languages and customs. But again, in the midst of this judgment, God had in His heart the day when He could bring all His people back together again. He wanted them to be united not in language, but instead in heart—that they would all have the same desire to love and honor Him, just as they were created to do.

Reflect

1. What was wrong with the people's desire to build this huge tower?

2. In what way did God judge the people?

3. Have you ever seen pride in your own heart? When?

Pray

Help us to remember, God, that we are Your people, and as Your people we should act with humility, seeking to honor You.

From Bad to Worse

Show

Rather than having an object lesson or game in today's portion of the story, explain that today you will look together at one of the most difficult stories in the entire Bible. The story of Job is a story full of mystery, of sadness, and of pain. But explain that it's also an important story because it can lead us to understand that God is in control even when it doesn't seem like it. As you begin, ask your family to think about some people in your family or in your church who are having a difficult time in life, perhaps due to sickness, job loss, or some other reason. Ask them to help you remember these people as you talk about the story of Job.

Read

Job 1:1–12

Explain

Unlike most of the rest of the Bible, we don't know exactly when these verses take place in the whole story. But we do know that it is one of the oldest stories in the Bible. Like Adam and Noah, Job was a man who lived a very long time ago. And the Bible tells us that like Noah, Job was a righteous man who believed and trusted in God. When God looked at Job, He saw someone faithful; but when Satan looked at Job, he saw something else.

Satan approached God and called Job's character into question, saying that the only reason Job was faithful and honoring to God was because he had such a blessed and comfortable life. In other words, Satan said Job loved and worshiped God not because of who God is, but because of what God had given Job. If all those aspects of his life changed, Satan argued, Job would turn away from God. And this is where the great mystery of Job comes into play: God allowed Satan to attack Job at every turn. Job lost his wealth, he lost his family, and he even lost his health. And yet the Bible tells us that Job did not sin in charging God with wrongdoing.

Today, we won't ever truly know the reason why bad things happen to us or to people whom we love. But we can know from this part of the story that nothing at all happens apart from God's plan, even when that plan is hard to understand.

Reflect

1. Why did Satan say that Job honored and obeyed God?

2. What is the difference between truly loving and honoring God, and just loving God for the good things He gives us?

3. Who are some people in our lives we can pray for today who are having a difficult time in life?

Pray

Lord, help us to accept that there are some mysteries we will not fully understand. But please help the people in our lives who are suffering to remain faithful even in the difficulties of life.

A Voice from the Whirlwind

Show

To illustrate the next section of the story, explain to the family that you will play a few rounds of the old game called "Telephone." This is the game in which you will whisper a phrase to one family member, and they have to whisper it down the line one at a time. Emphasize that they have to whisper quietly enough so no one else can hear what they are saying, and they only have the chance to say the phrase one time. Once you've played a few rounds of the game using some phrases of your choice, ask the family to think about what made the game hard, or what made it easy. If they were successful, then perhaps it was easy because the rest of the house was quiet. If they were not successful, then perhaps it was difficult because it was hard to hear clearly some of the words that were spoken. Explain that in today's story, we will see that Job wanted God to talk to him about what had happened in his life. And when God finally did, unlike the game you just played, Job had no trouble hearing God's strong voice.

Read

Job 38:1–11

Explain

When we last left the story, Satan was on his way from God's presence to attack Job's life. But despite everything that happened to him, Job did not abandon his faith. In the rest of the story, some of Job's friends tried to help, but they gave him bad advice. They said that the reason bad things were happening to Job was because he had done something wrong. But Job insisted on the truth, that he had remained true and faithful to God. All through his loss and through the bad advice of his friends, Job had a question for God: he wanted to know why the things were happening to him. So he asked God his question. And in Job 38, God spoke back to Job.

For several chapters in the Bible, God reminded Job of who God is. God reminded Job of His power and His wisdom. He is the God who created all things and holds all things together. Though God never answered Job's question about why these bad things were happening, God did help Job see that even when it doesn't seem like it, God is in control, and even bad things have a purpose in His wisdom. Today, we can remember the same thing, and we can choose to trust God even when it's difficult. In fact, we will see in the story that even on the darkest day, when it looked like everything in the universe had gone as badly as it could, God was still in control.

Reflect

1. What are some of the things we learn from the story of Job?

2. Why is it hard to trust God when life seems to be going badly?

3. What are some of the things we can remember about God to help us trust Him?

Pray

God, thank You that You are always in control. Help us to remember when times are difficult that You are powerful, wise, and loving.

Called to Go

Show

Position the family so that there is a bit of space between you and the rest of them. Explain that you will play a game of "Red Light, Green Light." The rules are simple: When you say, "Green light!", the family can move forward. When you say, "Red light!", they have to stop. But to make it more challenging, add an extra dynamic. For example, you might tell the family they have to crawl like babies or crabwalk. Then play a couple of rounds of the game. Debrief the experience by helping the family see that they were moving forward when you said to, and stopping when you said to. They were only allowed to go when you said so, and when you did, they moved immediately without hesitation. Explain that this game is meant to show what happened in the life of the next man we meet in our story, Abram. God told him to go, and Abram obeyed, even though he didn't exactly know when God would say stop.

Read

Genesis 12:1–4

Explain

When we left off in our story, all the peoples of the earth had been scattered. They were living in different places and speaking in different languages. But God still had in His heart a plan and desire to rescue all kinds of people from their sin. That's when Abram comes into the story. The Bible later tells us that Abram was a part of a people who worshiped many different gods. In fact, Abram's father made idols for his job. But Abram was different—he had chosen to believe in the one true God of the universe, and God had a very special plan for him. God had chosen Abram to be the person he was going to continue to tell his story through.

God made some serious promises to Abram. He promised to bless him, to protect him, that he would be the father of many nations through the years, and that all the people of the earth would be blessed through him. The first step for Abram was to go to a new land God was promising him. Though Abram didn't know it yet, he was to be the father of the nation of Israel, and it was through his descendants that God would finally provide rescue from sin and bless all the peoples of the earth.

Reflect

1. Do you think Abram was nervous when God said go? Why or why not?

2. What are some of the questions you might have had if you were Abram?

3. What do we learn about faith and obedience from Abram?

Pray

Thank You, God, that You still plan to bless all the nations of the earth. Help us to believe in You as Abram did and to show our faith through obedience.

Wait and Believe

Show

Gather together a black piece of construction paper and some salt in a shaker. As the family gathers together, shake out a generous amount of salt into the black piece of paper. Ask the family to consider whether or not they would be able to count the individual grains of salt on the paper. Though possible, it would likely take a long time to do so. But then ask them to consider if they had all the time in the world, whether they could count the individual grains of sand on an entire beach or all the stars in the sky. Emphasize that a task like that is impossible, but God did something like this with Abram to show him his future.

Read

Genesis 15:1–6

Explain

God had made big promises to Abram. He promised him a new land, many descendants and blessings, and that all the earth would be blessed through him. But though Abram was obedient to God and left his home to go a new land, he and his wife were getting older and they had yet to have any children. Abram had started to wonder whether God was serious about keeping His promises. After all, how could he be the father of many nations if he had not yet even had one son?

So God reaffirmed His promises to Abram. He took Abram outside and told him to look at the sky. He promised Abram that his descendants would number more than the stars in the sky. This very special kind of promise is called a covenant. Because God was making this covenant with Abram, it was dependent on God to keep it. Though it would take many years for God to fulfill His promise, Abram's job was simply to wait, obey, and trust that God would keep His word.

Reflect

1. Why was Abram wondering if God would keep His promise to him?

2. How can looking at the stars help us remember who God is?

3. Why is it hard to wait sometimes? What can we remember about God as we wait for Him to do what He promised?

Pray

God, we know that You keep your promises. Help us to wait for You to do what You've said You can do and to be obedient to You in the meantime.

The Price of Impatience

Show

Before gathering the family together, place a piece of candy or other treat for each one in front of you. Begin by telling them that you have this treat for them, but they will have to wait for it. Then just sit there in silence until someone breaks the silence. The point you are trying to make is that waiting is difficult under any circumstance, but especially difficult if you know there is something you want at the end of the wait. Ask the family to name a few times or places when it has been really hard to wait. They might mention things like waiting for Christmas, waiting at the pick-up line at school, or waiting to check out at the grocery store. Remind the family that God had given great promises to Abram, but Abram had been waiting for a long time. In today's part of the story, you will see what happened when Abram and his wife got tired of waiting, and the consequences that happened as a result.

Read

Genesis 16:1–10

Explain

Abram and his wife had waited for years for God to start ful-filling His promises. They were now more than eighty years old, and even though God had promised to give them a son, they realized that having a child was impossible. They were tired of waiting, and in their tiredness, they decided to take matters into their own hands. Sarai told Abram that he should try and have a child with Hagar, one of her servants. Abram agreed, and the child was conceived. But this was not the child of God's promise; this child was born out of a lack of faith. Even though Abram had showed his great faith in God, here we see an example of what happens when faith falters.

Though it was her idea, Sarai soured toward both Hagar and her son, Ishmael, and the two ran away. But God was merciful toward them, and made them some promises of their own. He would greatly multiply the children that would come from Ishmael, but as we continue to read the story, those descendants and the children of the promise would be in conflict with each other even to this day.

Today's part of the story is a reminder to us that part of faith is waiting and trusting that God will fulfill His promises in just the right way, and at just the right time. Bad things happen when we try and take matters into our own hands rather than waiting on God in faith. Many years later, we will see that Abram's children were also waiting—waiting for the promise of God's rescue to come true. And God would again deliver in just the right way, and at just the right time.

Reflect

1. What is the hardest part about waiting for someone or something?

2. Why did Abram and Sarai come up with a plan on their own?

3. What is our family trusting God to do that we are having to wait for?

Pray

God, help us to remember that You do just the right thing at just the right time. Help us to wait for You in faith.

She Laughs

Show

Explain to the family that you are going to have a laughing contest. The rules are simple: you can do anything except touch another person in order to make the members of the family laugh. Once you laugh, you're out of the game, and the last one who isn't laughing is the winner. After playing the game, gather the family together and explain that there are lots of reasons why people laugh. Sometimes we laugh because we hear or see something funny. Or we might laugh because we are happy at some piece of news we've just gotten. Of course, we might also laugh because we don't believe something, almost as a way of mocking the person who is telling us what we can't believe. It's this last case of laughter that we will see in the next part of the story.

Read

Genesis 18:9–15

Explain

The years stretched on, and with each year, Abram and Sarai were still childless. God had reassured them of His promise again and again, going so far as changing their names to Abraham and Sarah. These new names were meant to remind them of God's promise and the generations of descendants that were coming.

Then one day three visitors came to Abraham, and he recognized that these were not ordinary travelers, but instead messengers from God. They talked with Abraham, and they told him that in a year, he and Sarah would have a son. After all this waiting, the promise was only a year away! Though both Abraham and Sarah should have been overjoyed, Sarah was eavesdropping on the conversation, and rather than rejoicing, she laughed in disbelief. She knew how old she was, and she knew it was impossible for her to give birth to a child at that age. Sarah had failed to believe that what is impossible for men is always possible with God.

Today, we might have the same temptation. God has promised, for example, to return someday and fix everything that is broken in the world. We might look at the news, the wars, and the terrible things happening in the world today and laugh out loud at the thought that God can, and will, fix all this. But we should make sure to remember that God takes His promises very seriously, and because He does, so should we. A year later, the long-awaited child was born, and Sarah laughed again—but this time out of sheer joy. Abraham and Sarah named the boy Isaac, which means laughter.

Reflect

1. How should Sarah have responded when she heard this news?

2. What did she do instead?

3. Why is it important for us to remember that God takes His promises seriously?

Pray

Lord, thank You that You know every promise You've made, and You take them all seriously. Help us to do the same.

God Will Provide

Show

As the family gathers together, tell them that you had planned to bring cookies with you today to share. But since you didn't have any cookies, you substituted something else. At that point, take out a rock for every member of the family and give them the rocks instead of the cookies you failed to bring. As the rocks elicit a reaction from the family, ask them why they are upset. After all, you didn't come empty-handed—you brought a substitute for the cookies. Explain that a substitute is something that takes the place of something else. But further explain that not all substitutes actually fit and work. For example, the rocks didn't really take the place of the cookies. Point the family to today's portion of the story in which you will read together about a substitute that God provided. Remind the family that when you left the story, Isaac had been born after decades of waiting on the part of Abraham and Sarah. The boy began to grow, and today's part of the story takes place when Isaac was still young, perhaps a teenager, and God commanded Abraham to do something very strange.

Read

Genesis 22:1–14

Explain

God commanded Abraham to take his son, his promised and loved son, the one he had waited so long for, up the mountain and sacrifice him. Though we don't know how old Isaac was at this point, he was clearly old enough to travel, and even to help his aging father carry the supplies up the hill. Shockingly, we don't see any hesitation on the part of Abraham, though thousands of thoughts must have been running through his mind. But despite any doubt, fear, and sadness, Abraham showed the strength of his faith by trusting in God, and took his son up the mountain.

The altar was built, Isaac was laid upon it, and the knife was raised, but just as Abraham was about to plunge it down, he heard the command to stop. Abraham had showed his faith, and God was pleased. God provided a substitute for Isaac, a ram that would die in place of the boy. And in this story, we see a glimpse of the future, for thousands of years later there would be another Father who led another Son up another hill. This was the last sacrifice, the sacrifice that would end all the others. God the Father would sacrifice His own Son, Jesus, as a substitute for all who have faith in Him.

Reflect

1. What do you think Abraham was thinking as he went up the mountain with Isaac?

2. How did God provide what Abraham and Isaac needed?

3. What can we learn about God based on this part of the story?

Pray

God, thank You for providing exactly what we need when we need it. And thank You that You have provided the rescue from our sins in Jesus, our substitute.

Selling Your Future

Show

Gather together eight to ten objects from your home varying in value. These should be a great variety of items, from commonplace groceries (like a can of vegetables) to things that have sentimental value (like a photo album). Tell the family that they will have one minute to arrange the items in terms of their value. At the end of the minute, follow up by asking the family why they arranged the items as they did. Hopefully, they will have a little trouble with the more sentimental items because though they might not have cost a great deal, they are nevertheless very valuable. Explain that things in our lives have value not only because of how much you can buy or sell them for, but because of what they mean to us. In today's portion of the story, you will see together how one man misjudged the value of something he had and was willing to part with it.

Read

Genesis 25:27–34

Explain

Isaac grew up and married a woman named Rebekah, and they had twin boys they named Jacob and Esau. Esau was the older son, and in that time, the older son had more privileges than the younger. Esau, by the order of his birth, was entitled to a greater share of the family inheritance when Isaac died. But Esau took his birthright for granted, for one day he came home from hunting and his brother, Jacob, was making some stew. Esau smelled the stew and was willing to trade his birthright, something of great value, for a simple and much less valuable bowl of stew. For Jacob, he had shrewdly manipulated his way into receiving what was intended for his brother, though it damaged his relationship with him. God's promises would pass from Isaac to Jacob rather than to Esau, even though Esau was the older brother. He had sold his future for something of much less value.

We should be careful, even today, that we don't make the same mistake as Esau. Sometimes sin can look and feel so enticing that we are willing to trade our obedience and our relationship with God for it.

Reflect

1. What does this story show you about Esau?

2. In what ways might we be like Esau sometimes?

3. What do you think the relationship was like between Jacob and Esau from this point forward?

Pray

Lord, You have given us all such good gifts, and the best one is Yourself. Please help us not to trade in those gifts for things of lesser value.

The Stolen Blessing

Show

Gather five or six household objects of a variety of sizes and shapes, but all distinctive from one another. As the family gathers together, ask for a volunteer to play a game. Explain to the volunteer that you will blindfold him or her, and they will have to identify the series of household objects based on touch alone. Play the game and see how many objects the volunteer was able to identify. Talk about which objects were easy, and which were hard, and ask the volunteer how they were able to identify the ones they got correct. Then explain that as the story continues today, you will see together that Isaac was near the end of his life, and he wanted to pass on a blessing to his older son, Esau. But in his old age, Isaac was nearly blind. Rebekah and Jacob took advantage of the situation, and Isaac's blindness, to trick him.

Read

Genesis 27:5–17

Explain

In that day and time, the blessing was a very important part of family life. It was through the blessing that a father would pass down his authority to lead the family to the next generation. Traditionally, this blessing would be given to the oldest son—in this case, Esau. But Jacob and Rebekah once again wanted to manipulate the situation, and so they came up with a clever plan in order to trick Isaac into giving the blessing to Jacob instead of his brother. Through this deception, Jacob did indeed receive the blessing. Esau was understandably angry; in fact, the Bible tells us that he wanted to kill Jacob who first got his birthright, and now had received his blessing. But the Bible also tells us that even though these actions were deceptive and wrong, God was still working His plan. Surprisingly, God intended for the promise He made long ago to Abraham to go through Jacob and his descendants. Though hard to understand, this reminds us that the evil actions of men cannot stop the plan of God. God can even work through bad things to bring something good.

Reflect

1. How did Rebekah and Jacob trick Isaac?

2. How do you think Esau felt when he learned what happened? What about Isaac?

3. What does this part of the story remind us is true about God?

Pray

God, thank You that nothing can stop Your plan. Help us to remember that even when we see evil in the world today, we can know that You are still in control.

The Trickster Is Tricked

Show

To begin today's story, if you are married, show the family a few of your wedding pictures. If not, then consider using pictures of grandparents. As you show the pictures, have some fun remarking on the clothes of the time period, but also take time to tell the story of the first time you met your spouse. Be as descriptive as possible, and then transition to today's part of the story by explaining that the story is a love story. In this story, we see that Jacob ran away from home, fleeing in fear from his brother, Esau's, anger. He ran to some distant relatives, and when he got there, he saw Rachel and fell in love. But today's part of the story is not just a love story; it's a story of how Jacob, who had tricked others, got tricked himself.

Read

Genesis 29:13–25

Explain

Jacob agreed to work for his uncle, Laban, for seven years in exchange for the right to marry his daughter, Rachel. Jacob did the work, but when it came time for the marriage, Laban pulled a trick of his own. During that time, the brides wore thick veils, and Jacob did not realize that Laban had substituted his older daughter, Leah, in place of Rachel. The story goes on to tell us that Jacob agreed to work an additional seven years to marry Rachel, but he was so in love that the time passed quickly. Jacob now had two wives, but he loved Rachel more than Leah. The trickster had been tricked, but something else was happening. God was beginning to work in the life of Jacob to teach him what it meant not to rely on his own intelligence and ideas, but instead to trust in Him.

Reflect

1. Why did Jacob run away from home?

2. How did the trickster get tricked in this part of the story?

3. Why do you think God wanted to teach Jacob not to rely on himself?

Pray

Thank You, God, that we don't have to trust in our own ideas or intelligence, but instead can always trust in You.

Wrestling with God

Show

Tell the family that today you will have an arm-wrestling competition. One by one, arm-wrestle each of the family with the smallest child going last. In that arm-wrestling match, allow it to go on for a while making a show of how hard it is to win. Then, at the end, win the match. Then ask the family to consider whether or not they thought you would actually win every match. Of course, as an older and stronger person, you should easily win arm-wrestling matches with children. But then transition to today's portion of the story by explaining that if that is true of you, then how much more would it be true of God if He were in a wrestling match? In today's part of the story, you will see how Jacob left Laban with his family after having accumulated a great amount of wealth. He planned to go back home where Esau waited. But before he met his brother, there was another meeting he didn't know about it. At night, by the river, God waited for Jacob.

Read

Genesis 32:24–32

Explain

Jacob didn't know what to expect. He had been chased away from his home by his brother's anger, and after having been gone for many years, he was afraid that his brother's rage had not died down. The night before he would meet Esau, a "man" appeared and wrestled with Jacob. But this wrestling match wasn't about physical strength; it was about Jacob finally accepting God's authority and purpose for him. Though God could have overpowered him at any time, He wanted Jacob to understand who was really in charge.

During this wrestling match, God changed Jacob's name, signifying that Jacob should have a new identity; he was going to be a different kind of person as a result of the wrestling match. He had lived his life trusting in himself, but he would now walk through life differently, marked by faith in God who fights for His people. Jacob would now be called Israel, a reminder of his new identity. This same God who fought with Jacob is the God who fights for us when we are willing to give over our lives for His purposes.

Reflect

1. Why do you think God wrestled with Jacob all night, though He could have won easily?

2. What lesson was God trying to teach Jacob?

3. What would Jacob be reminded of because of his limp?

Pray

Help us, God, to accept and surrender to You. Help us to remember that You will fight for us when we choose not to fight with You.

The Dreamer and the Slave

Show

To introduce this section of the story, take turns amongst the family sharing the strangest dreams each of you has had. After everyone has had a chance to share, explain that in the Bible, dreams were often a means by which God relayed information and communicated with people. When we last left Jacob, he had been given the new name of Israel. And he went on to have twelve sons. He loved one of his sons more than the others, a boy named Joseph. Because Joseph was his favorite, Israel gave him a beautiful, multicolored coat which made Joseph's brothers very jealous. To make matters worse, Joseph had dreams that meant his father and brothers would someday bow down to him. Things came to a head one day when his brothers saw Joseph coming toward them.

Read

Genesis 37:18–28

Explain

The brothers' jealousy had turned to rage, and when they saw Joseph coming, they decided to kill him. One of his brothers, Reuben, was able to convince the others not to kill Joseph but instead to throw him in a pit. They did just that, but then when a caravan of traders passed by, the brothers decided they might be able to make some money off of Joseph. They sold him as a slave, and he was taken to Egypt. Meanwhile, the brothers soaked Joseph's coat in blood and told their father Joseph had been attacked by an animal.

The brothers were rid of Joseph, his father thought he was dead, and Joseph was transported to a foreign country. His life had been turned upside down—from being the favorite and privileged son to a slave in a foreign land. But as we'll see, God had not abandoned Joseph. In fact, Joseph's move to Egypt was part of God's plan to save His people. When unexpected things happen in life, we can be tempted to despair. We can feel abandoned, mistreated, and forgotten. But it's important to remember at those times that even if everyone else forgets us, God does not. And God can use even the worst parts of our lives in His story.

Reflect

1. Why did Joseph's brothers hate him so much?

2. What do you think Joseph was thinking as he was being taken to Egypt?

3. How can the story of Joseph encourage us when bad things happen?

Pray

Lord, thank You that You are always in control. Help us again today to trust in You and Your plan when things happen in life that we don't understand.

Falsely Accused

Show

Use a box of cereal to open up today's portion of the story. Show the box of cereal to the family. Ask them what they would expect to find when they open up this box. Ask if they would be surprised if they opened the box and found grapes or rocks. That would be surprising because the outside of the box is supposed to clearly show what is inside the box. Explain that this is what the word *integrity* means. To say a person is a person of integrity means that a person's inside matches what you see on the outside. They don't act one way around some people and a different way when they are with others or by themselves. And in today's part of the story, we will see that even in difficult circumstances, Joseph acted with integrity.

Read

Genesis 39:1–15

Explain

Joseph had been sold as a slave, but God was with him. When Joseph got to Egypt, he was bought by a man named Potiphar, and God made Joseph successful. In fact, he was so successful and trustworthy that Potiphar put him in charge of everything that happened in Potiphar's household. Potiphar trusted Joseph because Joseph lived with integrity.

But Potiphar's wife wanted Joseph to break God's law. Joseph showed his integrity by remaining true to what he believed, but unfortunately, that didn't stop Potiphar's wife from falsely accusing Joseph of sin. Though Joseph had done nothing wrong, he found himself in prison as a result of this false accusation.

Joseph had gone from being a favorite son to a slave, then from a trusted household manager to a prisoner. His integrity and faithfulness to God had cost him, and the same thing might be true for us today. Being faithful to God and living with integrity will sometimes come at a cost, but even when it does, we can trust that God sees our hearts as well as our actions. God will take note of when we live with integrity even if doing so comes at a cost.

Reflect

1. What happened to Joseph after he was brought to Egypt?

2. Why do you think Joseph was able to continue acting with integrity, even when it kept costing him?

3. What are some ways you can live with integrity today?

Pray

Help us, Lord, to live lives of integrity even when doing so comes at a price.

A Dream Come True

Show

Distribute paper, pencils, and crayons to each family member. Ask each child to take a few minutes and draw a picture of what it is they want to do for work when they grow up. Ask each adult to also draw a picture of what they thought they were going to be as an adult. Allow each family member to show and explain their drawing, including the adults. Then explain that often, as children, we have an idea of what life will be like when we are grown up, but we are usually wrong. It's pretty unusual for a person to have the job they think they want when they are a child. Remind the family that Joseph had a dream about what his life was going to be like when he was older, but he did not know how it would happen. He had been sold into slavery, been an important person in Potiphar's house, then falsely accused and sent to prison. In prison, he was able to interpret the dreams of two other prisoners, but he stayed in prison until one of those prisoners was able to share with the leader of all Egypt that Joseph could interpret dreams. Pharaoh, the leader of Egypt, sent for Joseph, and Joseph was able to tell him what his own dream meant—that there was a dangerous time coming for Egypt in which there would not be enough food to eat, and Pharaoh should prepare for it. Joseph was about to see the dream he had years earlier come true.

Read

Genesis 41:33–45

Explain

Joseph was able to interpret a dream with God's help that meant there would be a famine in the land of Egypt, a time when there would be little rain and no crops would grow. But before the famine, there would be a time of great abundance, and Joseph told Pharaoh he should store up food during the time of abundance so the land would have enough during the famine. Pharaoh was impressed with Joseph's wisdom and ability from the Lord to interpret dreams, so Pharaoh put Joseph in charge of all of Egypt. What an amazing turn of events this was! Only a few hours earlier, Joseph was a prisoner, and now he was the second most powerful man in the land. The dream he dreamt earlier in his life was starting to come to pass.

Even more importantly, though, God was moving Joseph into a position of power not for his own benefit, but because God knew that a dangerous time was coming for the family of Abraham, Isaac, and Jacob. Joseph had an important part to play in the story, one he could only perform if he were in charge of the whole land. See, it was God who put Joseph in charge. God was working through Pharaoh, even though Pharaoh didn't know it. The Lord never stops working, both in expected and unexpected ways. We can be sure that God is always busy doing something, making sure everything is working out exactly as He planned.

Reflect

1. Do you think Joseph was nervous meeting with Pharaoh? Why or why not?

2. How did Joseph show both his wisdom and his commitment to the Lord?

3. Why did God move Joseph into this position of power?

Pray

Thank You, God, that You are always at work. Help us to trust in Your plan even if we don't see exactly how You are working it out.

The Reunion

Show

To begin today's portion of the story, ask each family member to answer this simple question: "Who is one person you haven't seen for a long time that you would like to see again?" Answers might be a friend who moved away, a grandparent or other relative, or a past teacher. After each person answers, ask them to explain why they chose that person. Then explain that in today's part of the story, a reunion took place between people who had not seen each other for a long time. But unlike the reunions we described, no one was either expecting or looking forward to this reunion. Remind the family that Joseph's brothers had no idea what happened to him. In all the time he spent in Egypt, life went on for the sons of Israel. Then the famine Joseph predicted would happen actually came to pass. Because of the famine, Joseph's brothers traveled to Egypt to try and buy some food for their families. Imagine how surprised—and afraid—they were to find that the brother they sold into slavery was now the second most powerful man in Egypt, and the one who controlled the food supply.

Read

Genesis 50:15–21

Explain

Joseph could have been very angry and bitter with his brothers. His dream had come true, and now they were kneeling before him, and he had the power to take revenge on them for what they had done. But Joseph instead extended grace and compassion to them. Why? Because of Joseph's faith. He knew that even though his brothers had greatly sinned against him, God had used even their sin for good, and because of that, he was able to forgive and reconcile with them.

This is good news for us today because there will be times when bad things happen. If we are confident in God and His plan, we will be able to forgive others, and also to know that God can bring good even out of the worst things. Joseph did, and his brothers left their homeland and moved to Egypt to be under the care and protection of their brother. And as we look forward into the story, we will see that many years later, people would betray one of their own, who was closer than a brother. And like Joseph, Jesus would forgive them as well and bring them under His care and protection.

Reflect

1. How do you think the brothers felt when they found out Joseph was in charge in Egypt?

2. How was Joseph able to forgive his brothers instead of being angry at them?

3. Why is it important for us to forgive others if we believe in God?

Pray

Help us, God, to be forgiving people. Help us to remember when it's hard to forgive others that You have forgiven us.

Multiplied, but Oppressed

Show

To introduce today's portion of the story, ask the family to consider a simple scenario. Ask them to imagine that you were going to give them a gift, but they have to make a choice. Either they would receive one million dollars today, or they would receive one penny today, but every day for a month the amount would be doubled. So today they would get one cent, then tomorrow they would get two more cents, then the next day they would get four more cents, and so on. Ask them which they would choose? They will likely be surprised to find out that if you took a single penny and doubled it everyday, by day thirty, you would have $5,368,709.12. The point of the illustration is that things can quickly multiply in a surprising way. It's true of pennies, but in today's part of the story, we will see it was also true of the Israelites. When we left the story, the children of Israel had moved to Egypt to join their brother, Joseph. While things were good and prosperous for a while, we will see today that this prosperity did not last as the people continued to grow in number.

Read

Exodus 1:5–14

Explain

God had promised Abraham long ago that he would have far more descendants than he could even count. The promise had started with one son, Isaac; but as the years went on, Abraham's children grew and grew. In Egypt, they grew even more, until a new ruler of Egypt who did not care about all the good Joseph had done for the land reigned. When he looked at the great numbers of Israelites, he saw them as a threat. He worried that someday the Israelites would turn on the Egyptians, so to guard against that he enslaved them. Their enslavement was brutal and oppressive, and many generations of Abraham's children would live under those terrible conditions. In fact, God's people would be slaves in Egypt for 400 years.

Surely during those 400 years, the promise God made to Abraham was often repeated in homes and families as the people tried to hang on to hope that someday God would deliver them. And He would. Though the wait was long, a deliverer was coming. This deliverer, who would be named Moses, was only a shadow of the greater Deliverer God had in mind. Though His people were slaves in Egypt for 400 years, all people are slaves to that which is even more powerful than the Egyptian taskmasters. All people are slaves to sin and death and need God to come through again with a lasting deliverance.

Reflect

1. How did the Israelites become slaves in Egypt?

2. How do you think the people might have tried to remain hopeful even as they were slaves?

3. How are all people enslaved? How does God provide deliverance from this greater slavery?

Pray

God, thank You again that You always keep Your promises in Your time. Help us to recognize the slavery of sin and to turn to You for deliverance.

A Deliverer from the Water

Show

Distribute pencils, paper, and crayons to each member of the family. Ask each person to draw a picture of the perfect babysitter. Be sure to include things like what she brings with her, what she's wearing, and any other details. After a few minutes, ask each family member to explain their drawing. They will likely point out things like games, activities, or snacks the babysitter has. Explain that though all those things are important, the most important thing a babysitter does is keep the children safe. Explain that in today's part of the story, you will read together about a very fine babysitter—a sister, in fact—who was committed to taking as good of care as possible for a very important little boy named Moses.

Read

Exodus 2:1–10

Explain

Remember that God's people had been slaves for 400 years. During that time, the ruler of Egypt was so concerned about the Israelites becoming so numerous that he put a terrible law in place. He declared that any Israelite baby boys that were born had to be put to death. But there was at least one family that would not abide by this law, and so when their son was born, they hid him to keep him safe. When they couldn't hide him anymore, they put him in a special basket and floated the basket on the river. They trusted that God would take care of him, but Miriam loved her brother so much and was so concerned that she kept an eye on him as he floated away. The little boy was found by Pharaoh's daughter, and she brought the boy into her home. His sister, who was watching, suggested Pharaoh's daughter might need one of the Israelites to help take care of the boy. And so Moses' sister was later able to help reunite Moses with his mother.

Moses, meanwhile, was adopted into Pharaoh's house, and he grew up just like one of Pharaoh's own sons. Even though the people had been slaves for 400 years, God had not forgotten them. Just as God was in control of Joseph's circumstances, putting him in the right place at the right time, God was doing the same with Moses. He was going to make sure His people found freedom, and He would use this adopted boy to make it happen.

Reflect

1. Why would it have been hard for the family to hide this baby for several months?

2. How did Moses' family trust God?

3. How did God take care of Moses?

Pray

God, help us to remember that You will always take care of us in just the right way. Help us also to remember that many times, You use us to take care of the people around us.

From Prince to Shepherd

Show

To introduce today's section of the story, ask your family to talk about their favorite superhero. Give each family member a chance to respond, each one telling why that superhero is their favorite. Then transition the discussion by posing the question of what would happen if one of you decided to dress like their favorite superhero. You put on a Spiderman, Superman, or Wonder Woman costume. Would you automatically become just like that person? Of course not. As much as you might want to be, you would still be just an ordinary person who is dressed differently. This is sort of like what we see Moses doing in the next part of the story. He had been adopted into the home of Pharaoh and grown up there, but years later he saw an act of injustice. He wanted to be a hero, and so he made a bad choice in his attempt to help.

Read

Exodus 2:11–23

Explain

Moses had the right idea. He knew it was not right for the people of Israel to be enslaved. He might have even thought he was going to be the hero who would lead the people to freedom. But despite having the right idea, he did entirely the wrong thing. Moses committed an act of violence himself, and soon his act of violence was discovered. He wanted to be the hero, but he ended up running away from Egypt in fear. He ran, in fact, to the homeland of the people who had first brought Joseph to Egypt. Moses had gone from being a prince of Egypt to a lowly shepherd in Midian where he lived for many more years.

We should remember that our role, as we seek to do the right thing, is not to try and take God's place as a hero. There is only one Hero in our story, and our job is to point people to that Hero and follow Him where He leads. As for Moses, he must have thought he would spend the rest of his life far away from Egypt. But God was not finished with him yet.

Reflect

1. What did Moses do that led him to run away from Egypt?

2. How do you think Moses felt about being a shepherd when he had once been a prince?

3. Who is the true Hero in our story?

Pray

Lord, help us to remember that our job is not to be the heroes, but instead to know, love, and follow the true Hero—the only One who can truly save us from our sin.

A Bush, a Fire, and a Name

Show

As the family gathers together, tell the story of how each child was named. Were they named after people? What caused you to choose the name that you did? What were the circumstances around the name? After you have talked about everyone's name, explain that even though our names might have great meaning to us, in the Bible, names are even more important. Someone's name, in our story, is the person they are. A name does more than identify someone in our story; it describes them. And in today's part of the story, Moses is going to be personally introduced to Someone with the most important name.

Read

Exodus 3:1–14

Explain

Many years passed as Moses was in Midian until one day, he came upon a sight he had never seen before. On a mountain, he approached a bush that was on fire but was not burning up—and that's when things got even more strange. A voice came from the bush, and the voice knew Moses' name. God spoke to Moses, and as He did, He repeated the promise He had made to Abraham so many years ago. God had not forgotten

His promise, and though 400 years had passed since the people were enslaved, He had not forgotten them either.

God told Moses that He had chosen him to go back to Egypt and lead the people out. But Moses was skeptical. Though God knew his name, Moses did not know God's name. Moses wanted to know whether this God, who had never spoken to him before, was really the God of the Israelites. He wanted to know whether this God was really powerful enough to do what He said He could do. So Moses asked God for His name. God responded with what might seem strange—He said His name is "I am who I am." In this name, God was answering Moses' doubts. He was telling Moses that He is present with His people and that He never changes. He is the same God who breathed life into the world, the same God who flooded the earth in judgment, and the same God who miraculously gave Abraham a child. And He still is.

Today, we still follow this same God who never changes, and is always present. Though Moses was scared, God promised He would go with Moses on this mission. The presence of God would give Moses the confidence and strength he needed to do what was before him.

Reflect

1. Why do you think Moses was unsure about this mission?

2. Why was it important for Moses to know God's name?

3. Why is it important for us to know that God never changes?

Pray

Thank You, God, that You still are who You are. Help us to know that we can still count on Your promises that we read in the Bible.

One True God

Show

Gather the family together and tell them you are going to play a few rounds of the game, "Would You Rather . . ." This simple game offers someone a choice between two alternatives, and they have to choose which one they would rather do. Though this game is usually played using two terrible alternatives, forcing someone to choose the thing that is less bad, you might consider playing the game with two great things. For example, would you rather take a vacation to London or Paris? Would you rather have ice cream or cookies? After a few rounds, explain that just as you had two things to choose from, Pharaoh did as well. God sent Moses to Pharaoh to offer him a clear choice. Time and time again, Pharaoh, in his hard-heartedness, chose not to believe in the power of the one true God and let the Israelites go.

Read

Exodus 5:1–9

Explain

The choice was clear. The one true God had issued a command, but Pharaoh would not listen. He would not let the people go. As a result, Moses, with the power of God, brought down disaster after disaster on the land of Egypt. The Nile River, the source of all life in the region, was turned to blood. Insects devastated the crops of the people. The sun was blotted out and the land became dark. Every living thing was afflicted with all kinds of sores. Each of these plagues was a powerful reminder to all Egypt that the many gods they worshiped—the god of the Nile, the god of the sun, the god of fertility, and all the rest—were not gods at all. And after each plague, Pharaoh had the choice again—he could either acknowledge that God was the true God and let the people go, or he could remain stubborn. And each time he chose his own way rather than God's, another plague would fall.

God was demonstrating that no person and no pretend god can stand against Him. God was, is, and always will be the one true God, and soon there would be no doubt any more, for God was going to do to the land of Egypt what the Egyptian rulers had done to His people.

Reflect

1. How did God show that He is the only true God?

2. Why do you think Pharaoh was so stubborn and would not change his mind?

3. In what ways might we be like Pharaoh and not change our minds?

Pray

You alone are God. Help us to be humble before You, always willing to do what You say is right instead of being stubborn in our hearts.

Pass Over Us

Show

To introduce today's portion of the story, ask the family to think about some of their favorite holiday traditions. For example, what are some things your family does around Christmas that might be unique? As examples are shared, ask the family if they remember why that tradition started in the first place, and take turns sharing these stories as well. Explain that in today's portion of the story, you will see the beginning of a tradition that is still practiced by millions of people all over the world. But even more important than that, you will see how God chose to deliver His people from slavery in Egypt, and how He pointed us to a future event when He would deliver all who believe from the slavery of sin and death.

Read

Exodus 12:21–28

Explain

Nine different times Pharaoh could have let God's people go, but each time he refused. Now Egypt lay in ruins, having suffered from the devastation of the plagues God sent. The time had come for the final judgment—the one that would ensure the children of Israel would go free. God would put to death the firstborn, whether human or animal, all across the land. But in His judgment, God provided a way for the Israelites to be saved. They would offer a sacrifice, and they would paint the doors of their homes with the blood. God's judgment would pass over these doors, and those inside the home would be spared.

It's important to see that the reason God would pass over them was not because they were the best people; it wasn't even because they were Israelites. In fact, if an Israelite family did not do as God commanded then their firstborn would die along with the rest. No, the only way to be safe was through the blood. It was for something else to die as a substitute for the firstborn. Just as God provided a substitute for Isaac many years earlier, and just as He provided a way of escape from judgment for Noah, He told the Israelites how they could be rescued as well. In His judgment, there was mercy, and there still is. Today, we are still saved by the blood of another sacrifice—not the sacrifice of a lamb, but the sacrifice of Jesus who is called the Lamb of God. When His blood marks our lives, we can be saved from God's judgment of our sin.

Reflect

1. How were the Israelites saved from God's judgment?

2. How does this point forward to Jesus?

3. How can the blood of Jesus mark our lives, as the blood of the lambs marked the doors of the Israelites?

Pray

Thank You, God, that in Your judgment there is still mercy. Help us to trust in Jesus, the Lamb of God, as the only way we can be saved.

Glory in the Waters

Show

As the family gathers, make two parallel lines with tape or other objects on the floor. Then lead the family in a simple game of "Cross the River." Ask the family to imagine you were on a walk in the forest when you came upon a stream that you had to cross. In this game, each family member must stop at the first line and then leap over the gap between the lines. Extend the space between the lines farther and farther until there is only one person left, who is the winner. Transition to today's portion of the story by telling the family that after the last plague, Pharaoh did let the Israelites go, and they marched out of Egypt in freedom. But it wasn't too long before Pharaoh had second thoughts and decided to pursue the Israelites with his whole army. Soon Moses and the Israelites stood with the army of Egypt at their back, and the large Red Sea in front of them. Unlike the game, the sea was far too wide and far too deep to cross. But God was not defeated; in fact, things went just as He planned, for He was going to again show everyone His power and glory.

Read

Exodus 14:15–28

Explain

The Lord protected the Israelites from behind to make sure the Egyptians could not come any closer. And then the people saw once again the power of the God of Abraham, Isaac, and Jacob as Moses stretched out his staff over the waters. Miraculously, the waters parted, and all of Israel walked straight across. What an experience that must have been, to be walking through the sea on dry ground while the waters piled up on either side, held in place by the mighty hand of God. The Lord not only saved His people; He also displayed His glory before the world. For centuries, people would tell the story of this God. They would stand in awe of the God of Israel because of what He did that day.

Today, we can trust that God will still act on behalf of His people. He will make a way where there is no way, and He will do it in such a way as to show His power and glory.

Reflect

1. How do you think the people felt when they saw the sea in front of them and the Egyptians behind them?

2. How did God display His glory for the world?

3. Why should the story of the Red Sea encourage us?

Pray

Thank You, God, that You are a God of power and might. Help us to trust You even when we can't see a way forward.

Bread from Heaven

Show

Take turns for each family member to share their favorite meal you have together. After each has shared, take turns sharing your least favorite meal. After everyone has shared, explain that food is one of the easiest things to complain about. When we see something on the table that doesn't taste good to us, it's tempting for us to gripe and complain about it even though it's what has been provided for us. In the same way we complain about food, the Israelites did, too. Even though God had provided a way out of slavery in Egypt for them, even though He had miraculously parted the Red Sea, the people started to complain very soon after they left Egypt.

Read

Exodus 16:11–16

Explain

Once again, the Lord provided. Each morning, the Israelites would walk out of their tents and find that food had come down from heaven. And as we continue the story, we see that the Lord did this every morning for forty years as the people lived in the wilderness. Each day they had what they needed, and the Lord provided it all.

The people named the substance manna. But this manna from heaven was just a foretaste of how God would provide for His people in the future. Today, we won't go outside and find bread in our yard, but that's because God has provided for us in an even better way. Jesus is called the true Bread of Heaven because He is truly all we need. Our hearts and souls can be satisfied with Jesus and Him alone, for He alone is what God has sent down from heaven to nourish us.

Reflect

1. Why is it so easy to complain about things?

2. How did the Lord provide for the Israelites?

3. How did God provide for us in Jesus?

Pray

Lord, You provide for Your people. Thank You that Jesus is the true Bread of Heaven that has come down to satisfy all our needs.

The Mirror and the Window

Show

Bring a mirror with you to devotion, and then take the family with you next to a window. To introduce today's part of the story, ask the family to consider what the two things—the mirror and the pane of glass—have in common, and what is different about them. Though the family might name many things, the most obvious similarities are that both of the objects are made of glass. But the difference between them is that you can see through the pane of glass, but the mirror is reflective. Tell them to keep this illustration in mind as you read today about what happened to the Israelites next.

Read

Exodus 20:1–17

Explain

The people of Israel had been chosen by God, rescued by God, and provided for by God. They were His people, and because they were His people, God would tell them the right and wrong ways to live. On the mountain, God gave ten basic commandments that the people were to follow because they belonged to Him. The first half of these ten commandments had to do with how the people would worship God; the second half of these commandments had to do with how the people would live and interact with each other.

Even as God gave these commandments, though, He knew that the people would not be able to follow them perfectly. Even when they were able to do the right thing, their hearts would still be filled with sin, and these commandments did not have the power to change anyone's heart. Even though these commandments were meant to guide the people in how to live rightly, they had a greater purpose: they were to function as both a window and a mirror. Just as you can see through a window, these commandments would show the people the holiness and perfection of God. And just as a mirror reflects back to you, these commandments would reflect the people's sinfulness as they failed to live them out perfectly. God was showing His people that they didn't just need commandments; they needed new hearts. Hearts that were pure and holy, just like His. And the only way for them to get a new heart is through faith.

Reflect

1. Did God think the people would be able to keep the commandments perfectly?

2. If not, why did He give the commandments to them?

3. How are we like the Israelites?

Pray

God, Your law is perfect and true. But in our sinfulness, we cannot keep it. Thank You for showing us both Yourself and ourselves in the law, and help us to trust in Your grace for a new heart.

The Calf of Gold

Show

Distribute pencils, paper, and crayons to the family, and ask them to draw a picture of their favorite animal. After everyone is finished with their picture, in a sarcastic way praise the picture itself for the drawing (i.e., "My goodness! A monkey! Well, Mr. Monkey, you have done such a great job with this picture. You're an incredible artist, Monkey"). Having done this a couple of times, ask the family to comment on what you are doing. Of course, what you are doing is ridiculous—you are offering praise to a created thing. Even more, you are praising a created thing that isn't even alive. Explain that as silly as this is, it is precisely what happens next in our story. Even though God had just given the Israelites the laws they were to base their nation on, they quickly turned and made an idol for themselves.

Read

Exodus 32:1–8

Explain

Having delivered God's law to the people, Moses went back up on the mountain where he stayed in the presence of God for forty days and forty nights. While he was there, God gave him many specific instructions for the people. Meanwhile, the people became impatient. They made the same mistake Abraham made when he had to wait for Isaac's birth, the same mistake Moses made when he killed the Egyptian, and the same mistake we often make today. Because Moses took a long time to come down from the mountain, the people got impatient and decided rather than wait patiently in faith, they had to do something themselves. So, they crafted an idol for themselves, bowing down to worship it, as if something they created with their own hands had any power.

This is what an idol is—it is anything we give the credit to that is rightly due to God. If we keep reading the story, we see that God was very angry with the people, and the only reason He did not destroy them for their evil act is because Moses prayed for them. Idolatry is serious business. We should be careful today to make sure we are not bowing down to anything other than the one true God.

Reflect

1. What did the people do when Moses took a long time to come down from the mountain?

2. What is an idol?

3. What are some ways to make sure we aren't worshiping idols in our lives?

Pray

Lord, You alone are God. You alone are worthy of our worship. Help us to quickly recognize any time we are creating an idol to worship instead of You.

Blinded by Glory

Show

As the family gathers together, explain to them that you are going to have a contest to see who can look straight into the sun for the longest time. (This is, of course, not really going to happen. Only introduce the idea for the purpose of the object lesson.) Hopefully, one family member will object, saying that they cannot look at the sun even for a short period of time. Affirm this thought, and assure the family you are not really going to look at the sun. Explain that if you did, the moment you look directly at the sun your eyes would get sunburned. Stare at it for just a little while longer and the eyes will be permanently damaged, even to the point of blindness. Explain that the reason you brought up this fake game was to illustrate today's part of the story. Just as we cannot look directly at the sun, Moses also could not look directly at the Lord.

Read

Exodus 33:12–23

Explain

While Moses might have asked the Lord for many things, he chose to ask God simply to know Him more. Moses wanted to walk deeply with God, and he wanted a promise that God would go with the people everywhere they went. Moses knew enough to know that the only way he could continue to lead the people, and the only way the people would be sustained going forward, was through God's presence. His presence was the most important thing. In response, God promised that He would go with them, and what a glorious promise that is!

We can have the same assurance today, that as we believe in God, His presence is always with us—in an even closer way than He was with Israel. But God also knew there was a limit to how close Moses could be to Him. Even though Moses was obedient, he was still a sinful man, and God will not have sin in His presence. Like looking at the sun, Moses could not look directly at God and expect to live. Sin and holiness cannot coexist together any more than light and darkness can. The only way we can truly be in the presence of God is through faith. It's only by faith that we can be made holy, not because of the good things we do, but because God can make us holy through Jesus.

Reflect

1. What did Moses ask of God?

2. Why did Moses want to make sure God would go with him and the people?

3. How can we have the presence of God with us today?

Pray

There is none like You, Lord. Thank You that through Jesus and the Holy Spirit, we can know that You will never leave us.

His Presence in Our Presence

Show

As the family gathers together, ask them to think about the ideal home they would build if they could do it any way they wanted. No doubt children will respond with all kinds of extravagant amenities—bowling alleys, movie theaters, basketball courts, video game rooms, etc. Give everyone a chance to share, then turn the question by asking, "Now, what if you were not building the house for yourself, but someone else. How would it be different?" Hopefully, you will come to the conclusion that while you might want a bowling alley in your home, it's really up to the person for whom the house is being built. Transition to today's portion of the story by telling the family that having led His people into freedom, God gave some instructions about a house. But this would not be any ordinary house—it would be put away and rebuilt every time the people moved. Further, this would not be a house for any man or woman, but instead a house for the presence of God. This house would be called the tabernacle.

Read

Exodus 35:20–29

Explain

God had very specific instructions as to how the tabernacle would be built. He wanted it to have a specific type of material, wood, length, width—everything was to be built exactly as He commanded. The reason it must be built just so is because God is holy, and He wanted to make sure that the tabernacle showed the people just how holy He is. But, as we see in the story, God had already equipped His people to do everything He commanded if they were willing to surrender to His will. At the same time, God wanted the people to know that He wanted not to be distant from them, but in their midst. He wanted His presence to be in their presence.

God has always wanted to live closely with His people, whether in the garden with Adam and Eve or here in the wilderness with the Israelites. Unfortunately, the main thing that keeps the people of God from living closely with Him is their sin, and their sin could not be taken away by a special kind of building. It could only be taken away by giving them a new heart. And someday, God would do more than merely have His presence dwell in a building; He would come to earth Himself so He could truly be God with us forevermore.

Reflect

1. What is the most interesting part to you about the structure God commanded the people to build?

2. What are some of the talents you have that could be used to help people come into God's presence?

3. Why is it important to know that God wants to live closely with us?

Pray

God, thank You that You are a God who wants to live closely with Your people. Help us to love being close to You.

Cloud and Fire

Show

Prior to gathering the family for the daily story, take a sheet of paper and make a rudimentary map on it of either the inside or outside of your home. Make some marks on it so the family can identify different landmarks, then put an "X" on the map to signify something on the inside or outside of the house. Be sure and not make the map too obvious to figure out. As the family gathers, show them the map and ask them what they think it is. Hopefully, after some discussion, they will be able to say that it is a map of your property. Then ask them what they think the "X" represents. Ask them what maps are used for, and why someone might need one. Explain that maps are used to help people find their way from one point to another. Remind the family that the Israelites were now in uncharted territory. They did not know the right way to go in order to get to the land God was bringing them to. But they did not have to be afraid because even though they didn't know where to go, God did, and He would show them. They only had to trust and follow Him.

Read

Numbers 9:15–23

Explain

God did not give the people a map; instead, He showed them the way to go with His presence. In the daytime, the presence of God looked like a cloud, and at nighttime, it looked like a fire. The people would simply wait for the cloud or fire to move, and then follow it wherever it went. See, God did not have to tell the people all the directions at once; instead, He only required they follow Him one step at a time.

The same thing is true today. God rarely gives us the whole map of our lives. Instead, He desires that we have faith and simply follow His direction one step at a time. God gives us these directions today not with a cloud or fire, but instead through His Word. We can trust that He knows the way we should walk even when it might seem mysterious or difficult to us.

Reflect

1. Do you think it was hard or easy for the people to follow God in those days?

2. How did God show His people the way?

3. How can we know where God is leading us today?

Pray

God, thank You that You have not left us on our own. Thank You that Your Word is good and true, and we can trust You to help guide our steps.

Jealous Brothers and Sisters

Show

To illustrate the next part of the story, show the family a Band-Aid. Ask them to tell you the last time each of them used a Band-Aid. After each person has had a chance to tell their brief story, point out that Band-Aids can be really good for some things, like scrapes on the skin. But ask them to imagine that one of them had a broken arm. Explain that you would not put a Band-Aid on your arm if the bone inside were broken because the injury was far deeper than just the skin. Further explain that often the things we say and do show there is something wrong deeper in our hearts. This was the case with Aaron and Miriam, Moses' brother and sister. As we read this part of the story, it might seem like a little thing they were saying, but the Lord is able to look deeper. He saw something wrong with Aaron and Miriam that was more serious than just their words.

Read

Numbers 12:1–13

Explain

Aaron and Miriam didn't just complain against Moses; they had jealousy in their hearts. They did not like the decisions God was making with Moses, and they thought they should be more

87

important than they were. Because the Lord saw their hearts, He knew the true source of their words, and God punished Miriam for her jealousy. But notice the difference between the way Moses acted and the way his sister did. Even though Miriam was complaining and jealous of Moses, Moses forgave her and even prayed for her. Just as Miriam's words revealed her heart, so also Moses' words revealed his heart, and his heart was humble and obedient to the Lord. We, too, should be careful of the way we use our words, but not just because words can be hurtful. We should understand that our words show what we are truly thinking and feeling in our hearts. Often, like Miriam, we need someone in our lives who will pray for us even when our hearts are sinful, and thankfully, we have Someone like that. Jesus is our advocate who prays for us even when our hearts are sinful.

Reflect

1. Why were Miriam and Aaron upset?

2. How did God punish Miriam for her sin?

3. How did Moses show the state of his own heart?

Pray

God, please forgive us for things like jealousy that are in our hearts. Thank You that we have Jesus who loves us and prays for us.

Scouting Out the Land

Show

As the family gathers together, tell them they will go on a brief scavenger hunt through the house. Give them a list of five or six household items that are a bit difficult to find—things like a $1 bill, a plunger, a specific pair of socks. Then give them a time limit to go and find the items and bring them back. Once the family returns, explain that in our story, the people had been guided by God to the edge of the new land. Now it was time for Moses to send some scouts into the land to see what it was like. And, as our story will tell us, the scouts came back with both good news and bad news.

Read

Numbers 13:26–33

Explain

When the scouts returned, they reported that the land was everything they hoped it would be. It was a good land, good for setting up cities and towns and growing food. This was the land God had promised it would be—a good home for His people.

But there was also bad news. The bad news was the land already had people in it, and they were big, scary people. Caleb, one of the scouts, was not afraid. He was not afraid even though the people were large with mighty weapons because Caleb knew God was on their side. He knew the people only had to follow God and He would fight their battles for them. Unfortunately, though, the rest of the people lost their faith. Even though God had showed Himself to be mighty and faithful time and time again, they did not trust Him, and they chose to turn back instead of going into the land. As a result, the people would have to wander in the desert for forty years. They had come right to the very edge of the land, but would not go in.

Like the Israelites, we have chances every day to exercise faith. We all meet challenges in life and must make the choice about whether we are going to continue to believe in the God who has been faithful to us. If we do, then we will show our faith by continuing to follow Him no matter where He leads us.

Reflect

1. What was the good news the scouts brought back from the land?

2. What was the bad news the scouts brought back from the land?

3. What decision did the people make, and what were the consequences?

Pray

God, You are both mighty and faithful. Help us to continue to trust in Your power and faithfulness and help us to show our faith by following You wherever You lead.

Water from the Rock

Show

Gather the family together and explain that you will play a brief game of "Simon Says." After you've declared a winner, ask the family to tell you what makes a person really good at playing Simon Says. Hopefully, they will point out that a person has to listen carefully and obey exactly what the instructions are. Explain that when a person is the leader in Simon Says, that person is trying to get the participants in the game to mess up. But it's not like that with God. When God gives instructions, He isn't trying to get us to mess up; instead, God has great purpose in every instruction He gives. In the next portion of the story, we will see some very sad consequences that happened when Moses did not follow God's instructions.

Read

Numbers 20:1–13

Explain

God's people had the bad habit of complaining. Every time you turn around, it seems, they were grumbling and whining. And while complaining is bad enough, what makes it worse is what complaining reveals about our hearts. When we complain, it shows that we don't trust the way God is providing for us, and so it was for the people.

It seems from the story that Moses was tired of these complaints, tired enough that he lost his temper. Though God told him exactly what to do, Moses chose to do things his own way. Just like complaining reveals something about our hearts, so also did Moses' anger reveal his own distrust of God. And tragically, the consequence for Moses' disobedience was that he would not be the one to lead the people of God into the Promised Land.

Rarely are our actions just about making a mistake. Our complaints, our anger, our frustration? These are actions that can show us our hearts. And every time we see them it's an opportunity for us to turn back to God and trust in Him all over again.

Reflect

1. How did Moses disobey God?

2. What were the consequences for Moses' disobedience?

3. What do your actions tell you about your heart?

Pray

Lord, help us to trust that You always have a reason for the instructions You give us. Help us to show that trust by obeying.

The Snake of Bronze

Show

Gather the family together outside and explain that you are going to play a brief game of "Freeze Tag." Explain that you're going to be "it," and if you tag one of the family, then that person must freeze. He or she will have to stay completely still until someone else comes and tags them, at which point they are unfrozen. After you play for a few minutes, gather the family together and ask them to debrief the activity. Ask the family what they had to do to be unfrozen. Explain that in order to be made better, each person had to trust in someone else. In a way, this is like what happened to the Israelites in the next part of the story, as they were complaining yet again.

Read

Numbers 21:4–9

Explain

Complaints, complaints, complaints. Even though God provided manna from heaven every morning, and even though God provided water even when there was none, the people still complained. And in their complaining they failed to acknowledge how much and how often God had been faithful and generous with them. As a result, God sent snakes into the camp, and not just any snakes—poisonous snakes. Every person who was bitten by a snake died, and the people realized their sin.

Often this is how it works in our lives—we are in a pattern of sin and God helps us see our sin through some consequence. When we see our sin, we should do just what the Israelites did, which is to admit our sin and ask God to forgive us. The way God showed His forgiveness to His people was by providing a strange way for them to be healed of the poison that was coming from the snake. If the people did what God said, and only what God said, they would be healed. Of course, we too have a poison within us. The poison within us is sin, and it's only through doing what God said that we can be healed. Jesus would be lifted up on the cross, like the snake, and it's only by looking to Him that we can be healed from the poison in our hearts.

Reflect

1. What was foolish about the people's complaints?

2. How were the people saved from the poison of the snakes?

3. How is this similar to how we can be saved through Jesus?

Pray

Thank You, God, for giving us the way that we might be rescued from our sin. Help us to do what You have told us to do and look to Jesus.

The Donkey Speaks

Show

Explain to the family that in the next portion of the story, the Bible tells us the Israelites encountered many different peoples as they wandered for forty years, and in many cases, they fought with them. Explain that many of these lands and peoples have names we might not know, so you are going to play a simple game called "Bible or Star Wars." You will say the name of a land and the family will have to tell you if it's from the Bible or Star Wars:

- Oboth (Bible)
- Mattanah (Bible)
- Kessel (Star Wars)
- Scarif (Star Wars)
- Jazar (Bible)
- Bespin (Star Wars)
- Bashan (Bible)

These were all lands the Israelites passed through during their forty years, and in each one, God gave them victory. He was keeping his promise to bless those who blessed them and curse those who curse them. In fact, the reputation of God and His people had spread so far that rulers were afraid of what would happen if the Israelites came to their land. One such ruler, Balak, hired a man named Balaam to put a curse on the Israelites.

Read

Numbers 22:22–31

Explain

It was a simple enough job. Balak was paying Balaam to put a curse on the Israelites, and Balaam was on the way to do it. But his journey was interrupted by a talking donkey, of all things. Though Balaam was mad at the donkey, the words of the beast revealed that he had saved Balaam's life. God would not have His people cursed, and He had shown Balaam His true power not only by causing his donkey to speak, but also revealing the angel that was ready to strike him down if necessary. As we keep reading, we see that Balaam did deliver a message, but it was not a curse. Rather, the man hired to curse Israel instead did only what God told him to: he gave Israel a blessing.

As we look at God's people, we see again that they are blessed and protected not because they were the perfect people, but because God had promised to do so. And He will keep His promises to us still, not because we are deserving, but because He is gracious.

Reflect

1. Why were the people of God blessed and protected?

2. What did Balak hire Balaam to do?

3. How did God deliver His message to Balaam?

Pray

God, thank You that You will protect and guide Your people. Thank You that nothing can stop You from doing what You have promised.

Blessings and Curses

Show

To introduce the next portion of the story, lead the family to discuss some of the most basic rules you have in your home: don't play in the street, make your bed, feed the family pet, and other things like this. After you have named a few of the rules, ask your family to consider why those rules are in place. Explain that none of those rules are in place because you do not love the family; in fact, they are there because you actually do love the family. Those commands are made out of love because you want to make sure your family is safe and happy. God's commands are like that—He gives us commands because He loves us. In our story, the people had wandered in the wilderness for almost forty years, and were coming back to the edge of the Promised Land. Moses was addressing the people for the last time, and he wanted to try and help the people remember the mistakes of the past so they wouldn't make them again in the future. He did this by reminding them of God's good commands.

Read

Deuteronomy 11:26–32

Explain

Moses made it very simple for the people. There were two ways they could go. They could either obey God and be blessed, or they could disobey Him and be cursed. Of course, the people would want to be blessed—who wouldn't? But unfortunately, as we will see, the people did not obey God. Just as they had in the wilderness, they would worship other gods over and over again in their new home. God would discipline His people out of love to try and remind them of the way they should live, but their big problem was not just in their behavior. It was in their hearts. The only way the people could truly be blessed is through obeying God's command to have faith.

Like the Israelites, we have a problem not just in our behavior, but in our hearts. Unless God cures our hearts, we will never be able to obey Him. Only through faith can people, both then and now, truly have a new heart and be free from the curse of sin.

Reflect

1. Why do you think Moses wanted to talk to the people before they went into the Promised Land?

2. Remember that Moses would not be going with them into the Promised Land. How do you think he felt as he was talking to the people?

3. How can we truly be blessed today?

Pray

Lord, the choice is before us as well. Help us to be obedient to Your call to faith in Jesus.

A New Leader

Show

Explain to the family that you are going to take a brief historical quiz together. You are going to say a name of a great leader from history, then the family has to say the name of the person who became the leader afterward:

- George Washington (John Adams)
- Winston Churchill (Anthony Eden)
- Alexander the Great (Philip II)
- Walt Disney (Roy Disney)

Point out that it's a very difficult assignment to follow someone who has been a successful and inspirational leader. We often don't remember the second person because he or she lived in the first leader's shadow, failing to measure up. As we come to the next portion of our story, we see that the time had come for Moses to die, and for a new leader to take his place.

Read

Joshua 1:1–9

Explain

Moses was more than a great leader; he was a faithful leader who walked and talked with God. Furthermore, he was the only leader the people of Israel had ever known. Talk about some big shoes to fill! But God had already chosen the next leader of Israel. It would be Joshua, the one who had been with Moses a long time. Joshua had watched and listened to the way Moses had led the people and talked with God. Joshua was also one of the original spies Moses sent into the Promised Land, and he and Caleb were the only two who trusted that God was powerful enough to give them the land even though there were people there. Still, it would take much courage and strength for Joshua to complete his assignment, so God reminded Joshua multiple times that He would be with Joshua. All Joshua had to do was to trust and obey.

Centuries later, there would be another leader who would have to trust and obey. And this leader would actually have the same name as Joshua, because Joshua can also be translated as Jesus. Jesus would have to be strong and courageous, for He, too, would have to lead people into the Promised Land. But the new Promised Land would not be Canaan; it would be eternity. Jesus would lead all who believe in Him to eternal life with God.

Reflect

1. How do you think Joshua felt taking over for Moses?

2. Why did God tell Joshua to be strong and courageous?

3. How can we be strong and courageous today?

Pray

Thank You, God, that we can know You are with us. Help us to be strong and courageous as we trust in Jesus who is our leader.

Unlikely Aid

Show

As the family gathers together for the story, invite them to play a game of "I Spy." The simple game involves one member of the family picking out something around them, and then saying, "I spy with my little eye something . . . (name a color)." The family takes turns guessing objects until the correct one is identified. Use a few rounds of this game to introduce the next portion of the story in which, once again, spies were sent into the Promised Land, this time from Joshua rather than Moses. Explain that the Israelites had come to the same moment they had forty years earlier, standing at the edge of the Promised Land, and once again spies were going in to scout out the way. As before, the spies found a good land filled with fierce people. But unlike before, they were detected in their mission by the people of the land.

Read

Joshua 2:1–14

Explain

The spies were on the verge of being captured. They were being pursued, and if they didn't find a place of safety and help, they would surely be caught and executed. They found that help in the most unlikely of places. Rahab, a woman with a reputation for sinning, offered them aid. Rahab had heard the stories of these people, how God had dried up the Red Sea before them and had fought battles in the wilderness on their behalf. She believed in this God and knew it was just a matter of time until her own land fell. Because she believed, she took action and chose to align herself with God and His people, and because of her faith, she would be saved when the people came in to take the land. It was surprising aid from a surprising source, but God loves to work through unlikely people.

Rahab is a reminder to us that God welcomes any into His family who will believe, no matter what their past is like. Rahab became part of the Israelite nation, and centuries later, she would actually be part of the family tree of Jesus Himself, showing us that God works through unlikely people in unlikely ways.

Reflect

1. Why did the spies need help?

2. What did Rahab do to help them?

3. Why is it important that we remember the story of Rahab?

Pray

God, thank You for welcoming any who are willing to believe. Help us to never look at people like they are too far away from Your love.

Rocks of Memory

Show

Gather together several items in your home of a symbolic nature (i.e., a wedding ring, a special picture, a favorite coffee mug). These should be items that are not self-explanatory in their meaning, but rather require you to tell the story of the symbol. Explain the meaning behind each one, and then explain to the family that symbols like this are important because they help us to remember. Every time someone asks what they mean, it gives us the opportunity to tell the story again, which helps us remember even more. Transition to today's portion of the story by telling the family that as the Israelites went into the Promised Land, God commanded them to do something similar to help them remember His faithfulness.

Read

Joshua 3:14–17

Explain

God had done it again. Just as He had parted the waters of the Red Sea some forty years earlier, He now parted the Jordan River for His people. They went across on dry land, reminding them that the Lord was going to fight their battles for them if only they trusted in Him. But after the people crossed the river,

God told them to take twelve rocks from the dry riverbed—one for each original son of Jacob—and set them up where they would camp. God wanted there to be a lasting reminder of what He had done for them so the people would not forget.

We, too, might tend to forget from time to time what God has done for us. Whenever we worry, are afraid, or wander our own way, it's because we have forgotten all God has done for us. And like the Israelites, we must look back to God's Word and read about who He is to help us remember. As we do, we will see the most important thing for us to remember is God sending His Son, Jesus, to die for our sins.

Reflect

1. How did God help the Israelites get into the Promised Land?

2. What does that action remind you of?

3. Why is it important for us to remember what God has done for us in the past?

Pray

Lord, we are forgetful people. Help us to fight the fear and anxiety in our lives by remembering Your faithfulness.

The Walls Come Down

Show

Gather together some home repair items like a hammer, screwdriver, nails, and saw. Place them before the family and tell them that today you are going to use these materials to bake a cake together. Allow for the family's reaction, and then help them verbalize why they were so surprised. Of course, these are not the right tools you would need for something like baking a cake. Specific tasks require specific tools. Now transition to the story by telling the family that the first challenge in the face of the Israelites as they crossed the Jordan River was a mighty city called Jericho. Jericho was famous in the ancient world for its enormous, strong walls. The people might have expected all different kinds of tools they would use to conquer the city—swords, battering rams, shields—but God gave them a very different battle plan.

Read

Joshua 6:15–21

Explain

God had told the people that they would simply march around the city for six days, and on the seventh day, God Himself would cause the walls to fall. It must have seemed like trying to bake a cake with home improvement tools. Imagine how much Joshua and the people had to trust God in order to obey His plan. Like Noah who built the ark, like Abram who left his home, like Moses who stood before Pharaoh, God once again required faith from His people. And God came through. He won the battle on behalf of the people, and He did so in a way that made it crystal clear that He deserved all the credit. Just as it was in those days, God still desires faith more than anything else from His people. When we trust God, He will fight our biggest battle for us—the battle against sin and death. And once again, He will provide the victory.

Reflect

1. What was strange about God's plan for the people?

2. How do you think the people felt as they walked around the city for days?

3. What does God desire from His people?

Pray

Lord, thank You for fighting and winning the battle. Help us to trust in You.

Almost Faithful

Show

    As the family gathers together, pose the following scenario to them. Let's say one of them was told to go and clean their room, so they went upstairs, they gathered everything in the room that was out of place, and they threw it all in the closet and shut the door. Then they came back and said they had done what was required of them. Ask the family to consider whether they were truly obedient or not. Of course, they were not, because even though the room might look clean at first glance, it was not—the mess was only hidden. Explain that this kind of partial obedience is really no obedience at all. Obedience is doing what you are told, when you are told to do it, with a happy heart. Anything less is less than faithful. Transition into the story by explaining that God had just won a tremendous victory on behalf of the Israelites at Jericho. The Israelites were commanded to destroy everything in the city. And most of them were faithful, but partial obedience is no obedience at all.

Read

Joshua 7:1–5

Explain

The Israelites were almost obedient. They were almost faithful to do what God told them to do. But "almost" faithfulness is not faithfulness at all. One man, Achan, did not trust that the Lord was giving the right command. He thought he knew a better way to live, so he chose to steal some of what was supposed to be destroyed at Jericho. As a result, the next battle—which should have been an easy one for the Israelites to win—was an embarrassing loss. The people almost lost heart. But God knew the truth of Achan's sin, and He exposed it before the community. Before that exposure, though, many people suffered as a result of this one man's choice. Sin has a way of doing that—it not only affects us, it affects the people around us. Many people feel the consequences for one person's sin.

Fortunately, the opposite is also true. Many people can also feel the result of one person's righteousness, and the greatest example of this is how many can be saved through the righteousness of one person: Jesus Christ.

Reflect

1. Why do you think Achan stole some of the items from Jericho?

2. In what ways might our sin affect other people?

3. How can our righteousness help other people?

Pray

Lord, help us to recognize that "almost" obedience is not obedience at all, and instead to follow You with our whole hearts. Thank You for Jesus, whose righteousness saves us.

God of Time

Show

As the family gathers together, ask them to brainstorm an activity. Each person will have to complete the following sentence: "If I had one more hour in the day, I would . . ." Allow each family member to complete the sentence, then explain that while it's fun to imagine what we could do with more time, the amount of time in each day is set. The Lord has made the times and the seasons to pass by with regularity, and we measure the passing of the time by the sun. But it's also important to remember that even though the Lord has set up the times and season to pass with regularity, He still controls it all. In fact, in today's portion of the story, we will see the Lord exercising that control over time.

Read

Joshua 10:9–14

Explain

Despite an initial defeat at the city of Ai, the Lord was faithful to His people, and after they repented of their disobedience, He again gave them victory. There was a group of people in the land, the Gibeonites, who had made peace with the Israelites. But now those people were being attacked, and they called to Israel for aid. Joshua went to help them because the Lord had promised again to give Israel victory, and that's when the miraculous happened.

The Bible tells us that God did three things for Israel. He threw their enemies into confusion, He rained hailstones down upon them, and then He caused the sun to stand still in the sky so the Israelites could continue the battle. Think about that—God actually stopped time for a period for the sake of His people. This is yet another reminder to us not only of the power of God over all things, but also the lengths God will go to because He loves and is faithful to His people.

Reflect

1. Why did the Israelites go into this battle?

2. How did God help the Israelites?

3. How should this part of the story encourage us today?

Pray

God, You are Master over all things, even time. Help us to trust in Your power and to trust that You are committed to the good of Your people.

Over and Over Again

Show

Gather together several pieces of different games and place them before the family (dice, game pieces, a game board, playing cards, etc.). Explain that today you will play a game together using these pieces. Rather than giving any rules for the game, just say, "Go!" Observe what happens for the next couple of minutes and then lead the family to see that without rules, there was chaos. No one knew the purpose of the game, how to win, or even what moves they were supposed to make. One family member could play a version of the game and win it in their own eyes without anyone ever really playing along. Explain that this kind of chaos is a little like the period that happened next in the story. Joshua led the people faithfully and they took possession of the Promised Land, but after Joshua died, another generation came up that did not remember God or the things He had done for Israel. They began to live not under God's rule and authority, but rather according to whatever they wanted. These were the days of the judges.

Read

Judges 2:11–19; 21:25

Explain

The days recorded in the book of Judges contain some of the most entertaining stories in the Bible. People like Gideon, Deborah, and Samson were enabled by God to do incredible things, but despite these great stories, the overall message of Judges is one of sadness. It's the part of the story in which Israel, time and time again, abandoned the worship of the one true God. They would worship idols, God would try and get their attention by bringing oppression into their lives, they would return to Him, God would raise up a deliverer for them, and then the whole thing would start over again. Over and over again it was this same pattern.

Though they performed great deeds, ultimately none of these judges we read about had the power to change people, because the problem with Israel wasn't just their sinful actions; it was their sinful hearts. This pattern reminds us that we need a greater judge—a greater hero—the ones we read about in this book. We need someone who can do more than change our circumstances; we need someone who can change our hearts.

Reflect

1. What, in your own words, were the days of the judges like?

2. What was the people's real problem?

3. How does God solve that bigger problem?

Pray

God, as we read this section of the story, help us to remember that our biggest need has to do with our hearts and not our circumstances.

The Left-Handed Benjamite

Show

Distribute pens and paper to each member of the family. Tell them that you are going to have a writing experiment designed to test the family's penmanship. Ask each person, as neatly as possible, to write their full name on their piece of paper. But before they begin, ask them to use the opposite hand of their dominant hand to write. It should be interesting to see people struggle with using their opposite hand to do the writing. Then transition to today's portion of the story. Explain that the character you will meet in the story today did something with his opposite hand that no one expected, and because he did, he was able to help God's people regain their freedom.

Read

Judges 3:12–30

Explain

The people of Israel were unfaithful to God, and as a result, God allowed Eglon, king of Moab, to have power over them. But the people cried out to God and asked for help, and God raised up a deliverer named Ehud. In those days, everyone fought with their right hand. Knowing this, Ehud came up with a clever plan to hide a knife on his opposite side. When he was searched for weapons before going in to see the king, the soldiers only searched the side of him on which they expected to find a weapon. But because Ehud had trained to fight with his opposite hand, he was able to sneak the knife past the guards. Ehud killed Eglon in secret, and then was able to escape and lead a rebellion against Moab.

Even though the people had not been faithful in worshiping God, God still provided a way of deliverance for them. This is something we will see over and over again in this part of the story, that God is faithful to His people even when they are not faithful to Him.

Reflect

1. What is the most interesting part of Ehud's story to you?

2. How was Ehud able to sneak the weapon past the guards?

3. Why is it important to remember that God is faithful to His people even when they are not faithful to Him?

Pray

Lord, You are good to Your people. Thank You that Your faithfulness does not depend on our faithfulness.

The Help of a Friend

Show

As the family gathers together, ask each one to think of a task they would not want to do alone. The answer might be as simple as going down to the basement of the house or maybe some kind of physical exercise like going on a run. Allow each family member to share, and then acknowledge that many times when we have to do something that is difficult or frightening, it's helpful to have someone go with us. Explain that today we will meet someone who felt that way, and fortunately for him, he had someone to go with him.

Read

Judges 4:1–10

Explain

The cycle of the judges had begun. The Israelites would begin to worship idols, then God would bring about difficulty in their lives, they would plead for His help, and God would deliver them. At this time in the story, the judge leading Israel was named Deborah, and she had a message for Barak, one of the Israelite commanders. God had already commanded Barak to go up and attack King Jaban's army, but Barak did not want to go. This was a frightening assignment, and even though God told him to do

116

it, Barak was still hesitant. He wanted someone to go with him. And while Barak should have had enough confidence because God had told him to go, Deborah agreed that she would go too.

We also have been given orders by God. We can read messages from Him any time in the Bible, but many of the things God tells us to do are difficult or even scary. This is one of the reasons why it's important that we are around other Christians, so we can do these things together. Of course, we can know that no matter who goes with us, we will always have a friend who is closer than a brother in Jesus. He will always be there, no matter where we are and no matter what we do.

Reflect

1. Why should Barak have already done what God said?

2. Why did he ask Deborah to come with him?

3. Why is it important that we have friends who believe the same things we do?

Pray

Thank You, God, for giving us the gift of each other. Help us to remember that it's our job to help each other follow Jesus, no matter where He tells us to go.

The Not-So-Mighty Warrior

Show

As the family gathers together, show them a basketball. Tell the family that today you are going to do something incredible. You are going to take the basketball, jump from the free throw line, turn a flip in the air, and then dunk the ball. No doubt there will be objections from the family at something so impossible. Ask them why they are skeptical, then explain that someone told you that you were a great basketball player, and so you must be able to do this. Again, there should be objections from the family. Transition to the story by acknowledging how ridiculous it is to think you could do that just because someone said you were a great player. But further explain that if God was the One who told you that, then surely you would be able to do it. That's what happened in the next part of the story.

Read

Judges 6:11–16

Explain

Israel had once again turned to their idols, and the Lord had once again caused a foreign people to oppress them. The Israelites were being treated so badly by the Midianites that they were hiding from them in caves and in the mountains. One of the hiding Israelites was Gideon; he was so afraid of the Midianites that he was preparing his crops in a wine press, hiding what he was doing for fear the Midianites would steal his wheat. The angel of the Lord called Gideon a "mighty warrior," a very strange title considering where Gideon was and what he was doing. But things are what God says they are. And just as God was able to speak everything in the universe into existence, he was able to tell Gideon exactly who he was.

In the same way, when we believe in Jesus, God says some things about us. He says that we are His sons and daughters, that we are dearly loved children, and that we will be co-heirs with Jesus. He says this even though bad things still happen to us: we get sick, get a bad grade on a test, miss the team we're trying out for, lose a loved one, and have all kinds of other troubles. We need to remember that we are who God says we are no matter what our circumstances might be.

Reflect

1. Why was Gideon hiding?

2. What is so strange about what the angel called Gideon?

3. Why is it hard sometimes to remember who God says we are, if we believe in Jesus?

Pray

God, thank You that You are bigger than our circumstances. Help us to remember that we are Your sons and daughters.

Too Many Soldiers

Show

To illustrate today's part of the story, place a board game in front of the family with all the pieces displayed. Explain that you'd like them to play the game. But before they start, tell them you think they have too much equipment, and take away one of the game's elements, like a game piece or the dice. Continue this pattern until it would be impossible for them to play the game because you've taken too many pieces of it away, and then tell them it's time to play. Obviously, the game can't be played because you have taken away what they needed to do it. Explain that this is kind of what happened to Gideon as he got ready to fight the Midianites.

Read

Judges 7:1–8

Explain

Though he was initially frightened, Gideon eventually agreed to do what God commanded him to do, and he even rallied an army to go and fight the battle with the Midianites. Imagine Gideon's surprise, and even panic, as God stripped down his army. What started out as a strong group of soldiers was eventually trimmed to only three hundred men, a small group compared to the size of the Midianite army. While it might have looked like an impossible task to Gideon, God wanted to make sure that when the victory was won, there would be no doubt that God was the One responsible for the victory. He chose to make Gideon's army small and weak so He could show just how big and strong He was, and in doing so, gain the glory from the battle.

The Lord went on to defeat the Midianites using Gideon and his small band of soldiers, and when it happened, everyone knew just where the credit should go. This is how God chooses to work. It's not usually through the smartest or the strongest or the most talented people; instead, it's through our weakness, so He can show His strength.

Reflect

1. What happened to Gideon's army?

2. How do you think Gideon felt as he saw the size of his army decreasing?

3. Why did God choose to work in this way?

Pray

Lord, thank You that You are strong when we are weak. Help us to trust in You when we feel weak, knowing that our weakness is an opportunity to see Your strength.

The Strong Man

Show

Explain to the family that you are going to have a push-up contest, and allow each family member to do as many push-ups as they can. After each person has competed, declare the winner. Explain that there is a limited number of push-ups for everyone, even though some people can do more than others. No one can do push-ups forever, because eventually everyone's strength runs out. In today's part of the story, though, you will read about one of the judges who seemed to have a limitless supply of strength and power. But as we will see, even this man's strength had its limitations.

Read

Judges 14:5–7

Explain

Once again, the Israelites had done what was evil in the Lord's sight, and once again, another group of people oppressed them. This time, it was the Philistines, and the Israelites were under their control for forty years. But then God raised up another deliverer named Samson. Samson's parents made a vow on his behalf that Samson would have a special commitment to God—he would be set apart in his actions. As a result, God gave Samson incredible strength to do incredible things. Yet even though Samson was strong, he never really acknowledged the source of his strength. Rather than being humble before God, Samson was proud. He assumed his strength would always be there, and he used his strength not for God's glory but instead for his own.

Though the story of Samson has some amazing moments, it is a warning to us. Samson is a reminder to us that the source of our talents, strength, and blessings is God, and we should not take advantage of those, but instead live humbly before Him and acknowledge where the source of all good things come from.

Reflect

1. How did Samson show his strength?

2. What was the source of Samson's strength?

3. How should Samson have chosen to live?

Pray

Lord, help us to live humbly before You. Guard our hearts from pride and instead help us to acknowledge that You are the source of all good things.

True Power

Show

Display before the family an unplugged lamp. Ask the family if they know how a lamp produces light, and then allow them to try and explain how the process works. Then turn the knob and comment on how nothing happens, asking the family why not. Then explain that the lamp, in and of itself, does not really have the power. It must be plugged into the power source, and if that connection is broken, then the lamp cannot produce light. Explain that as the story of Samson continues, we will see that Samson finally had to pay the price for not recognizing the true source of his strength.

Read

Judges 16:4–6

Explain

Samson had done amazing things. He had torn a lion apart with his bare hands. He had fought and killed many Philistines, as many as a thousand with the jawbone of a donkey. He had caught three hundred foxes and used them to burn down a village. He was able to do all these things not because of his own strength, but because God was the source of his power. And yet in all these things, not once did Samson humbly thank God or give God credit for his strength.

When Samson met and fell in love with Delilah, he was very sure of himself. So sure that he was willing to play games with her, even though she tried several times to get him to tell her how his strength could be taken. Part of Samson's vow to God was that his hair would never be cut, and eventually he told this to Delilah. But even the hair was not the true source of Samson's strength; it was merely a symbol of what God had given him. When his hair was cut, so also his vow to the Lord was broken, and Samson at last was taken prisoner by the Philistines.

God's power is not to be used for our own ends; rather, God empowers His people to be on the same rescue mission He is on. He empowers us to glorify Him and to share the good news about Him with others.

Reflect

1. How do you see Samson's foolishness in this story?

2. Was Samson's power in his hair, or in something else?

3. What are some of the warnings we learn from Samson?

Pray

God, thank You for empowering Your people to be on the same mission You are on. Help us to have the same commitment You do to the rescue of people.

One Last Time

Show

As the family gathers together, ask them to think about their favorite "underdog stories." Examples might come from books, movies, or sports. The point of the exercise is for everyone to have a chance to share about someone who should have been defeated, but against all odds, came out on top in the end. Transition to today's portion of the story by explaining that Samson had lost his strength. He had gone from being the favorite in every battle to the underdog. In fact, the Philistines considered him as good as dead. But as we will see, God was not finished with Samson.

Read

Judges 16:21–30

Explain

Samson had gone from being feared to being mocked. Here, at the end of his life, he was weak, enslaved, and blind. He was even a source of entertainment for the very people who were once so afraid of him. And yet here, finally, we see the first glimpse of humility from Samson. This is the first time we see him acknowledge who God is and the source of the strength he had for much of his life.

And God heard Samson. As it turned out, Samson was not a lost cause after all. He showed faith in these last moments of his life, and God responded to him. Even though Samson had wasted much of his life, God was still merciful to him, and that is important for us to know in this story. The Bible is full of people who might be considered lost causes, but God loves and uses all kinds of people who make mistakes as long as they are willing to come to Him humbly in faith.

Reflect

1. How do you see a change in Samson's attitude at the end of his life?

2. How did God respond to Samson?

3. How should that encourage us?

Pray

Lord, help us to remember that no one is out of the reach of Your grace and mercy. Help us to humbly and quickly come to You when we make mistakes.

Wherever You Go

Show

Gather the family together and play a simple game of "Follow the Leader." Allow each person in the family to have a brief turn, and then after each does, ask the family to explain the rules of the game. The rules are, of course, very simple—you simply have to go wherever the leader goes in the way they choose to go there. Use the game as a jumping-off point into today's part of the story. Remind the family that God had led His people to take possession of the Promised Land, and for many years, the people had been in the cycle of disobedience, oppression, deliverance, brief obedience, and then disobedience again. During this time, God had used people like Gideon, Deborah, and Samson to judge and deliver them. It was during this same period that some new characters come into the story: Ruth and Naomi. Ruth was married to Naomi's son, but both women's husbands had died, and the women had to decide what to do next.

Read

Ruth 1:11–18

Explain

This was a hard situation for many reasons. Naomi was an Israelite who had two sons, and both sons had married women from another nation while the family was living there. But now Naomi's husband and both her sons were dead, and in that time, women often had to rely on the charity of others if they did not have a husband. Naomi and her daughters-in-law had a very uncertain future. Naomi decided to go home, back to her own people, and Ruth had to decide what to do next. Though she would have been a foreigner in the land, Ruth nevertheless followed the leader—she committed to stay with her mother-in-law. What an amazing display of loyalty and sacrifice! Ruth could have chosen to go back to her own people, to her own family, but instead she remained committed. What she would find was that God still had some of her own story left in His mind.

Reflect

1. Why was life difficult for Naomi and her daughters-in-law?

2. Why was it a sacrifice for Ruth to stay with Naomi?

3. What does this story teach us about commitment?

Pray

Father, thank You that You will never leave or forsake us. Even when times are difficult, we can trust that You will always be by our side.

A Redeemer Emerges

Show

Lead the family to the refrigerator and open it. Ask them to look at what's inside, and come up with the best meal they can think of using only the leftovers, without opening any new food. Allow each person to have a shot at creating their meal, then comment about how fortunate we are to have the ability to have fresh food. Imagine if we could only eat the leftovers from someone else all the time. But that's just the situation Ruth was in. Without a husband, she had no one to work and earn money for the home, so she would have to take what was left over. But in today's part of the story, we will see how God provided for her even then.

Read

Ruth 2:2–12

Explain

Ruth and Naomi were back among Naomi's people, the Israelites, but they still had to find out how to live. Ruth proposed the idea of picking up the leftovers from the grain harvest, and when she was there, she was spotted by Boaz. Boaz already knew something of Ruth—he knew of her kindness, her mercy, and her care for her mother-in-law—and Boaz extended a similar kind of care and compassion toward her. In fact, if we continue reading the story, we will see that eventually Boaz actually became Ruth's new husband.

Ruth's story started with tragedy, but the Lord did not lose sight of her. In her need, He provided for her. Boaz was Ruth's redeemer—someone who rescues another and pays a price for doing so. And if we read even further, we see that Ruth and Boaz had children of their own, and one of their distant grandchildren would be the true and greatest Redeemer, the One who rescues every person from sin and death.

Reflect

1. How did Ruth find a way to help her and her mother-in-law survive?

2. How did God provide for Ruth?

3. What are some ways God still provides for us?

Pray

You, Lord, are the great Provider. Help us to be obedient to You, trusting You will provide all we need in due time.

The Last Judge

Show

Ask every member of the family to share their favorite gift they have ever received. Ask them to share not only what the gift was, but why they wanted it, and how long they had to wait for it. After everyone has had a chance to share, explain that as our story continues, we meet a woman who had a great desire. But she didn't desire a house or a piece of clothing or anything like that; she wanted a child.

Read

1 Samuel 1:9–20

Explain

The period of the judges was soon to draw to a close. Hannah, a faithful woman who worshiped and trusted God, lived a life of sadness because she was unable to do the thing she wanted most: to have a child. Still, in the midst of her sadness, she prayed to the Lord and made a vow that if God would give her a child, she would give that child back to God. One of the things we learn from Hannah's story is that God cares deeply about those who are poor, hurt, and in need just as Hannah was. He paid attention to Hannah's humble prayer and gave her what she desired.

Hannah did indeed have a son, and she named him Samuel. Just as God has a special place in His heart for those among us who are in the greatest need, so also should we pay special attention to those around us who are in need. We cannot turn our eyes away from the poor and the mistreated around us if we are truly following God. Samuel, as his mother promised, would be dedicated to the Lord. He would be the last judge and would usher in the days of the kings of Israel.

Reflect

1. What do we learn about prayer from Hannah's story?

2. What do we learn about God from Hannah's story?

3. What are some ways we can make sure to pay attention to those around us who are in need?

Pray

Father, thank You that You are close to the brokenhearted. Help us to follow Your example and care for those who are in need.

Actions and Consequences

Show

To begin today's family devotion, present the family with either a deck of cards or a set of dominos. Ask them to use either the cards or the dominos to build a house. What will likely happen is that at some point, the house they build will collapse. Use the collapsing house to transition into today's portion of the story. Explain that at the time Samuel was born, a man named Eli was the priest in Israel, along with his sons. While their family was meant to help the people worship and honor the Lord, the sons of Eli were not faithful. They were using their positions for their own gain instead of serving God and the people. But like the house of cards, their family would soon collapse. Their actions had consequences, and those consequences would be severe.

Read

1 Samuel 2:12–17

Explain

When the people brought a sacrifice to the Lord, they were to bring their best. Doing so was an act of faith and worship—it demonstrated that the people recognized God deserved the very best, and He would provide everything they needed even as they sacrificed to Him. But these priests were taking the place of God.

They were selfishly and greedily taking the best for themselves. The house they built would tumble like a stack of cards; in fact, if we keep reading, we see that Eli and all his sons would eventually be killed. But even as God executed this judgment, He promised that someday a new priest would come. This priest would honor God fully, and He would lead the people to do the same. The new priest would be the same One who would rescue the people from their sins by offering the greatest sacrifice—Himself.

Reflect

1. What was wrong with what Eli's sons were doing?

2. Why was God so angry about these actions?

3. What would be the difference between Jesus and these priests?

Pray

Lord, help us to remember that You deserve the best. Thank You for our Priest, Jesus, who offered the very best sacrifice.

Your Servant Is Listening

Show

Lead the family in playing a few rounds of the game "Marco Polo." Explain that one person is going to be "it," and the rest of the family has to hide somewhere in the room. The person who is "it" will be blindfolded or close their eyes, and will have to feel their way through the room trying to tag someone. The people in the room can move around to avoid being tagged; but each time the "it" says "Marco," everyone must respond by saying "Polo" and give away their position. The game ends when the "it" is able to find and tag someone. After you play a few rounds, explain that this game is based on a call and response. Everyone had to respond in an appropriate way, and in this case, the response is the word "Polo." Explain that in the same way, there is an appropriate way to respond to the call of God. We will see the right response in the next part of the story.

Read

1 Samuel 3:1–10

Explain

The sin of Eli and his sons was not unknown to God, and He was going to remove them from their position as priests in the land. At the same time, God was raising up a new servant named

Samuel. He would communicate with Samuel so Samuel could deliver God's Word to the people. Samuel, even as a boy, began to hear the voice of the Lord, but he didn't recognize it at first. Eventually, though, Samuel responded in the way he should. He took the posture of listening to God's Word and then acting on what he heard.

We must do the same thing today. God has given us His Word, and it's found in the Bible. When we approach the Bible, we should approach it humbly, in the same way that Samuel did. We should trust that God will speak to us through His Word, and our job is not to talk but instead to listen and obey.

Reflect

1. Why was Samuel confused at first?

2. What was the right way for Samuel, and us, to respond to God's Word?

3. Why might it be hard to listen to God's Word sometimes?

Pray

Lord, as we open Your Word each day, help us to do so with listening ears and willing hearts.

No Lucky Charm

Show

To prepare for the family devotion, find a pair of the oldest, dingiest socks you can. Explain to the family that this is your lucky pair of socks. Ask them to examine the socks, and then ask them what they think would happen if you wore those socks today? Allow them to answer in some fun ways, but in the end, make sure and point out that these aren't really lucky socks. That's because there is no such thing as lucky socks. But then explain that the Israelites, in a way, believed they had a lucky charm. They treated the ark of God like this pair of socks, that if they had the ark of God, then nothing bad would happen to them. But as we will see in today's part of the story, God's presence is not some kind of charm that we can use to make things go the way we want.

Read

1 Samuel 4:1–11

Explain

The Israelites had been defeated by the Philistines, and they had been defeated badly. But as they returned from their defeat, they thought they had the answer. The ark of God, which God told them to build many years earlier and which housed precious things like the commandments of God and some of the manna from the wilderness, was with them. They thought they could use the ark of God like a magic charm to defeat their enemies. But the ark was not a lucky charm; rather, it was a symbol of God's desire to be in the midst of His people. Tragically, when the people trusted in the ark as if it had power on its own, they were not only defeated again, but the ark was captured by the Philistines. It was a dark day for Israel because the ark was gone, and with it the people must have wondered if God had abandoned them.

We should be careful that we don't treat the things of God like this. We should be careful not to think that if we read the Bible, we will have a good day, or if we always go to church nothing bad will happen to us. If we believe this, we aren't really loving God; instead, we are using God to get things we want. Fortunately for the people, God had not abandoned them. Eventually the ark would return to where it belonged, a reminder of God's enduring faithfulness—but not before the people moved even further from their relationship with Him.

Reflect

1. What was wrong with how the people viewed the ark of God?

2. What happened as a result?

3. How might we make the same mistake as the people?

Pray

God, help us to remember that You are not some kind of magic charm we can use to get what we want. Help us instead to love and worship You.

Give Us a King

Show

Ask your family to imagine that you worked all day on a special dinner. All day you chopped veggies, you baked bread, you baked cake, you grilled meat, and finally at dinner you put the whole meal down before them. And when you did, all the kids took one look at the meal before them and demanded something else. Ask the family to consider how that would make you feel? Point out that you would probably be angry and hurt, not because the family rejected the food, but because of something bigger. They weren't just rejecting the food; they were rejecting you as the one who had made it. Ask the family to keep that in mind as you read together the next part of the story.

Read

1 Samuel 8:1–9

Explain

Up to this point, God had done incredible things for His people. He had called Abraham to go to a new land to start this people. He had delivered them from Egypt, provided for them in the wilderness, given them victory as they took the Promised Land, and fought for them time and time again when they asked Him to. Through that time, Israel had various leaders like Moses,

Joshua, and the judges, but they never had an earthly king. That wasn't because God forgot to give them a king; instead, it was because God Himself was their king. But now the people were asking for something God had chosen not to give them. They wanted a king they could see, like all the rest of the nations. But they were not just asking for a king; they were choosing to reject the King they already had.

As we will see, God would give them what they wanted. Their first king would be named Saul. But even as God gave them the king they wanted, He would remind them that all their earthly kings would fall short of their true King. Their true King was still to come.

Reflect

1. What was wrong with the people's request?

2. Why do you think God gave them what they asked for?

3. How can we show that God is our King?

Pray

Lord, help us to remember that our true King is Jesus. Help us to worship and follow Him above all others.

Halfway Obedience

Show

Tell the family that you are going to demonstrate how to peel a potato. Show them the potato and the potato peeler, then peel about half of the potato and sit it down before them, and claim that you are finished. Hopefully this will elicit a reaction. Argue with the family a bit when they say you're not finished, claiming that you are. But then explain that the job was to peel the potato. You did half of the job but doing half of the job isn't the same thing as following all the way through. Explain that this was kind of like the way Saul was as king. He would "sort of" obey the Lord, but he rarely did everything just the way God commanded him to. Over and over again, Saul failed to completely obey the Lord, and as we will see today, it finally cost him.

Read

1 Samuel 13:6–14

Explain

Saul could have continued to wait on the Lord. He knew the right way to do things because God had commanded that sacrifices be offered in a certain way, at a certain time, by a certain person. But in order to do things the right way, he had to continue to wait. And in order to wait, he had to have faith.

Saul saw the desperate nature of the situation, knew the troops were frightened, and panicked and took matters into his own hands. This was the last straw, and God declared He was raising up a new king, a king with a different kind of heart.

Like Saul, sometimes we can get impatient when we're waiting on the Lord and decide to take things into our own hands. This never turns out good. Even when we think we're doing what's best, when we act apart from God's direction our actions come from pride (thinking we know better than God) and a lack of faith (not believing He'll make good on His word).

Reflect

1. How did Saul show his lack of faith?

2. How should Saul have responded instead?

3. What kinds of things can we learn from the life of Saul?

Pray

Lord, help us to act in faith even if it means waiting. Forgive us, Lord, when we take matters into our own hands.

Heart Matters

Show

Distribute paper, pens, crayons, and markers to the family. Ask each person to draw a picture of a king. After a few minutes, ask each person to explain the different parts of their picture. In most cases, the kings will be tall, handsome, nicely dressed, and have a crown. Affirm that these are pictures of what we typically think a king looks like. Explain that Saul actually looked like this kind of king. He was tall, handsome, and powerful. He looked every bit of a king on the outside, but his heart was far from God. The new king would be different in almost every way.

Read

1 Samuel 16:1–12

Explain

One by one, Jesse's sons were marched before Samuel. And one by one, Samuel thought he had seen the new king. Samuel was doing what we all typically do; we look at the outside of a person and think we know and understand them. But God looks at the heart. The youngest son of Jesse didn't look like a king; he didn't sound like a king; he wasn't the right person in the family to be a king. But he had a heart that loved God, and he was the one God had chosen to be king.

David would be the great king of Israel, and yet even David would fall. There was still another King to come. Like David, He would not have the appearance of a king, but His heart would be completely pure and devoted to God.

Reflect

1. Who was the new king that would come after Saul?

2. What was surprising about God's choice of the new king?

3. Why is it important for us to remember that God looks at the heart?

Pray

Help us to remember, Lord, that You look past outward appearances. Help us to care more about the heart than the outside as well.

Into the Court

Show

As the family gathers together, ask each family member to give you a different part of speech. For example, you will need someone to name a noun, someone to name a verb, and others to give adjectives and adverbs. Once you have all the words, challenge the family to make up a song using all those words. Give them three minutes to complete the song, and then ask them to sing or say it. Affirm that composing music is difficult; it's an extraordinary talent to be able to compose music and lyrics, especially ones that are memorable. Further explain that David, in addition to being the next king of Israel, was also a musician. Music would be an important part of his life and one of the reasons we still remember him.

Read

1 Samuel 16:14–23

Explain

When we last left David, he had been chosen to be the next king. But even though God had chosen him to be king, he was still just the youngest son of Jesse, a shepherd working for his father. But in God's plan, Saul came to know about David because he was a musician, and Saul needed some music in his life to help him feel better. It was because of David's music that he first came to know Saul, and first came into the court of the king.

One of the things we learn from this is the fact that God will use our natural talents for His purposes. We might not realize it, but all the things God has gifted us to do can play a role in God's plan. We should be open and ask how God might want to use our abilities for His kingdom.

Reflect

1. How did David come to be a part of Saul's court?

2. What does this teach us about God and His plan?

3. What are some of our talents that God might use for His plan?

Pray

Thank You, God, that You made us each unique and special. Help us to use our talents in order to glorify You.

The Giant Killer

Show

Bring a tape measure as you gather together for family devotion, and explain that you are going to read one of the most well-known parts of the story this morning—this part of the story involves David and a giant named Goliath. Explain that the Bible tells us, among other things, that this giant was almost ten feet tall! To demonstrate the true size of Goliath, stand on a chair and measure ten feet from the ground. Allow the family to see the scope of the giant, then continue to explain that the reason we should know how big Goliath was is not so we can be impressed with him, but be impressed with God's power.

Read

1 Samuel 17:41–52

Explain

David had come upon a scene which required action. Day after day, the Philistine Goliath had been challenging the armies of Israel. Even worse, he was insulting the God of Israel in his arrogance. Goliath's challenge was simple: instead of the entire armies fighting each other, Israel should send out one man to face him. The loser's people would become slaves to the winner's people. While the rest of Israel was afraid to face Goliath,

David was compelled to do so for the glory and honor of God. He did not need armor; he did not need more strength; David knew that he only needed to trust in God.

In a most unlikely way with the most unlikely of weapons, David defeated Goliath. And while on the one hand this is a story about how we don't have to be afraid because God is on our side, it's also a reminder of a greater battle to come. Many years later, Jesus would face the enemies of sin and death on behalf of all humanity. And He, too, would defeat that enemy with the most unlikely of weapons—the cross.

Reflect

1. What was Goliath's challenge to Israel?

2. Why did David feel compelled to fight Goliath?

3. How does the story of David and Goliath remind us of Jesus?

Pray

God, thank You that You are bigger than any foe. And thank You that in Christ, You have defeated the greatest foe on our behalf.

True Friends

Show

Ask the family to share the names of each of their closest friends. After everyone has shared, ask each person to name three characteristics of someone who would make them a good friend. Again, allow everyone to share, and then explain that everyone needs friends. This is how God made us, and that included David. David had been anointed as the next king of Israel, he had been brought into Saul's court, and he had won a great victory over Goliath. He also came to know Jonathan, Saul's son, and the two became great friends.

Read

1 Samuel 18:1–5

Explain

In today's portion of the story, we see that Jonathan not only said he was David's friend; he showed it. He gave David important gifts, and he also made a covenant with David. We have seen that word *covenant* before, when God made a covenant with Noah and then Abraham. A covenant is a serious promise—one that is to be kept forever. And that's just what Jonathan did. Not once, but twice does the Bible tell us that Jonathan loved David as much as he loved himself, and this is the mark of a true friend.

A true friend is someone who wants the best for you, even if it means personal cost to themselves. And though Jonathan was a great friend to David, his covenant points us to the greatest friend we will ever have. Jesus loved us enough to die for us and to rescue us from our sins. He is a friend that is closer than a brother, one willing to give everything for our sake.

Reflect

1. How do we know that Jonathan was David's friend?

2. What can we learn about how to be a friend from Jonathan?

3. How does Jesus show that He is our friend?

Pray

Thank You, God, for the people You have placed in our lives to be our friends. Help us to be the kind of friends who are willing to sacrifice for others, and thank You that we have the greatest example of friendship in Jesus.

A Jealous King

Show

To prepare for family devotion, gather a variety of small foods together. There should be some that are sweet, like a small piece of candy, and some vegetables like a carrot stick. Using tape, fasten the foods underneath the chairs where the family will sit. When the family arrives for devotion time, ask everyone how they're doing, then invite them to look under their chairs, and comment on what each one finds. Ask the family to consider how they feel about what they found, and hopefully you will receive some responses that indicate that some wish they had what someone else had. Explain that just a few seconds ago, everyone said they were doing fine, but now everyone feels something different. Transition to today's part of the story by explaining that Saul felt something like this. Though he was at first glad to have David around him, he started noticing what David had that he did not.

Read

1 Samuel 18:6–16

Explain

David had made quite a splash in the kingdom. Suddenly, Saul no longer felt grateful for the young man who played music for him, had won battles on his behalf, and was his son's best friend. Saul began to feel jealous, and the jealousy began to eat away at his heart until finally he even tried to kill David.

This is how jealousy works in our lives; it begins with just a thought when we see someone who has something we don't have, but then it grows inside of us until somehow we express it on the outside. This is not how we are meant to live. The opposite of jealousy is contentment, and contentment is fueled by faith. When we believe God is in control of what we have and what we don't have, we can fight back jealousy. And when we know how much God has given us by adopting us into His family through Jesus, we realize just how much we already do have. It's only through Jesus that we can celebrate the victories of others instead of longing for them to be ours instead.

Reflect

1. Why was Saul jealous of David?

2. Do you ever get jealous? When?

3. How can we fight jealousy in our hearts?

Pray

Father, help us to be content with what You have given us. And above all, help us to remember the greatest gift: Jesus.

Protect and Serve

Show

Bring a common, household product in a package to the family devotion time, making sure that the item has some type of "warning" label on it. Present the item to the family, then point out the warning label and read it to them. Ask the family to consider why the warning label is there. Obviously, a warning label is put on a product to help the person using it to know of any danger it might present. Explain that this is something a friend does—they help keep us out of danger. But further explain that a true friend doesn't just keep us from danger; a true friend seeks our good. A friend both warns and advocates for us, just as we will see Jonathan did for David.

Read

1 Samuel 20:35–42

Explain

David knew Saul was seeking to kill him, but Jonathan was not so sure. He found it hard to believe that his father would do something like this. So the two friends came up with a plan by which Jonathan could warn David if he was indeed in danger. Sure enough, Jonathan heard from his father's own mouth that Saul wanted to kill David, and Jonathan made good on his word to warn his friend. The warning would come through a signal Jonathan would give.

Jonathan chose to protect David, his friend, even though it meant going against his own father. He was committed to doing the honorable thing no matter what the cost. But Jonathan didn't only warn David; he wanted David's good. Jonathan knew the Lord was with David, and so the two swore to each other not only to be kind to each other, but also to show that kindness to their future families. Jonathan once again shows us the true nature of friendship. And once again, we are reminded that in Jesus, we have a friend who not only warns us from the danger of sin, but One who actively seeks our good.

Reflect

1. Why did Jonathan have trouble believing David was in danger?

2. How did Jonathan show his friendship to David?

3. How does Jesus both warn us and seek our good?

Pray

Thank You, Lord, that You love us enough to give us warnings. But thank You that You also love us enough to seek what's best on our behalf.

The Good Shepherd

Show

To introduce today's portion of the story, ask the family to put together a job description. Explain that a job description is a record of the kind of work a particular person does. Ask them for some specific aspects that might go on a job description for a shepherd. Then remind the family that among other things, David was both a shepherd and a musician. In fact, many of the songs he wrote are recorded in the Bible in the book of Psalms. Today you will read together David's most famous song, Psalm 23, and in the psalm, David likens God to a shepherd.

Read

Psalm 23

Explain

We don't know when David wrote this song, but perhaps he wrote it as a young man, while he was tending his father's sheep. At this point in David's life, though, he was on the run from Saul. If indeed David wrote this song as a young man, you can imagine him singing it to himself, finding comfort as he was hiding from the angry king that God was looking after him. In the song, David notes all the things a good shepherd does—he cares for the sheep; he protects them from harm; he guides them to good places. These are all things David would have needed done for him during this period of his life.

For centuries, people have looked to this psalm for comfort as a reminder that even on the darkest days of life, God is their shepherd. If we believe in Jesus, then we become like the sheep of God's pasture, and we can rest assured that God is our Good Shepherd who will take care of us.

Reflect

1. What are some of the things a good shepherd does, according to this psalm?

2. Is this psalm for everyone or only those who believe in Jesus?

3. Why is that important to remember?

Pray

God, thank You that You are the Good Shepherd of those who trust in Jesus. Help us to trust in Your care, guidance, and provision even when we don't understand what is happening around us.

In God's Time

Show

Bring two objects to the family devotion time today—a cookie and a carrot (you can substitute other objects; the point is to bring one that is desirable and one that is not). Place both objects in front of one member of the family, and then ask him or her how long they think they could sit and wait to eat the cookie. Ask the same question about the carrot. Likely, they will respond they could wait much longer to eat the carrot than the cookie, because the cookie is something they really want. Explain that David ran from Saul for a long time—perhaps as long as ten years. Remind the family that David had already been anointed as king, so he knew that eventually the throne would be his. But as we will see in today's part of the story, David was willing to wait on God's timing, knowing that God's timing was the right timing.

Read

1 Samuel 24:1–15

Explain

Saul was right there before him. Defenseless and unaware. David saw the man who was trying to kill him, and the man who stood between him and the kingdom of Israel. All he had to do was sneak up a little bit further and take Saul's life and all the running and hiding would be over. But David didn't, even though his men wanted him to. That's because David knew that God had chosen Saul to be king for the time being. He further knew that to take Saul's life would be a sin against God, and David was not willing to take the throne of Israel in a sinful way. Instead, he would exercise faith. Unlike Saul who, as we saw before, took matters into his own hands instead of waiting on God, David waited on God instead of taking matters into his own hands.

Any time we have to wait for anything, it requires faith. We must believe that God's time is right, and that if we take matters into our own hands to get what we want, then it will never work out in the end. Centuries later, Jesus would walk the earth. He, too, had been promised a kingdom, and He would have many chances to take that kingdom by force. But like David, Jesus trusted in the Father's plan and was willing to wait for just the right time.

Reflect

1. Do you think it was hard for David to let Saul go? Why?

2. Why did David let him go instead of killing him?

3. Why does it take faith for us to wait on God's timing?

Pray

Thank You, Lord, that You are always on time. Please help us to wait for You to accomplish Your purposes in just the right way and at just the right time.

The Throne Passes

Show

As the family gathers together, ask them to play a game of "Hot Potato." The simple rules are that the "potato," which can be any object, starts in the hands of one family member and they have to pass it to another while music is playing. The game continues until the music stops, and the person left holding the potato is out. Play the game until there is a winner. Then remind the family that God had chosen Saul to be the first king of Israel. During that time, the next king would have been Saul's son, and the throne would have stayed in the family. But because of Saul's disobedience, God had chosen to pass the throne to someone else. In the story today, we will see the throne pass from the family of Saul to the family of David.

Read

2 Samuel 2:1–12

Explain

While David was busy running from Saul, Saul was not only chasing David; he was also contending with other enemies like the Philistines. And in a fierce battle that took place on a mountain, the Israelites were defeated, and Saul and his family were killed, including Jonathan. The time had come, just as God said it would, for the throne of Israel to be taken from Saul's family and given to David's. David was free to take the kingdom. He could come out from hiding. He no longer had to run. But in a moment when we might think David would be relieved and happy, he was not. He was deeply saddened at the loss of the king and his friend Jonathan. David did not think about his own gain, but instead mourned the great loss. In this, we see the attitude that we are to have as we follow Jesus. We are to think of others as better and more important than ourselves, putting them first, just as Jesus did for us.

Reflect

1. Why might David have been celebrating?

2. Why was he mourning instead?

3. What do we learn from this about the way we should treat others?

Pray

Lord, You have showed us how to live in relation to others. Help us to put others first as we follow Jesus.

The King Is Here

Show

Gather together a piece of string, and something much stronger like a piece of rope or a chain. Show the piece of string to the family and ask them if they think it's very strong. Explain that on its own, the string is easily broken. But then wrap the string around the chain, and explain that this is what happens when we trust in God. We are weak like the string, but we become united to God when we align with His purposes. We will see today that David was weak like the string, but because he was committed to God, he became very strong.

Read

2 Samuel 5:1–10

Explain

The time had come. Many years had passed since Samuel anointed David. There had been years of battles, of running, and of waiting, but now the next king of Israel was ready to take the throne. David brought all the people of Israel under his control and even took the city of Jerusalem. All this happened not because David was strong, but because the Lord was with him. David would be a great king, and he would reign forty years. But he was a great king primarily because he was a man after

God's heart. We do not need to seek greatness on our own, but instead, should focus on living in such a way that we, too, can be people after God's own heart.

Reflect

1. How do you think David felt when at last he was king?

2. Why was David able to be such a great king?

3. What does it mean to be a person after God's heart?

Pray

Help us, Lord, to be the kind of people who love You more than anything else. Help us to be people after Your own heart.

 **Day 4**

Precious Cargo

Show

Bring two boxes with you to family devotion. Ask two members of the family to pick up one box each and move it across the room and back. Then take a strip of tape, on which you have written the word *fragile*, and put it on one of the boxes. Ask the family to consider how moving the fragile box would be different than moving the other box. Obviously, you would be more careful with the box marked fragile because you assume what's in the box is precious or breakable. Explain that as David became king, he knew it was important to bring the ark of God to Jerusalem. But the ark was precious cargo—unfortunately, David was not careful enough.

Read

2 Samuel 6:1–11

Explain

The ark was a holy thing because of the presence of God. And nothing unholy could touch it. This is why God was very specific with His people about who could enter His presence, and how the ark was to be handled. Unfortunately, David seemed to be so excited about moving the ark to Jerusalem that he neglected these instructions.

We might tend to have the same reaction as David, thinking that this was too harsh of a punishment when Uzzah was only trying to keep the ark from falling. But instead of this reaction, we should take this as a reminder and a warning about the seriousness of God's holiness. We should be very careful about approaching God, knowing that the only way we are safe in His presence is if we have been forgiven and made right by Jesus.

Reflect

1. Why was the ark being moved to Jerusalem?

2. What happened on the way?

3. What does this show us about coming into the presence of God?

Pray

You are a holy God. Help us not to be too casual as we think about You and approach You. Help us to remember we are only safe because of Jesus.

The Dancing King

Show

Ask the family to have a dance party for a few minutes. Choose some music to play, and then ask each member of the family to dance to the music for thirty seconds. No doubt some family members will be self-conscious and reserved; this is actually the point of the illustration. After each person has had a chance to perform, ask them to reflect on whether or not they thought they danced with all their might. Explain that it's often difficult for us to do something like dancing, even around family, because we are concerned about what others will think of us. But, as we will see in today's part of the story, David was so overcome with joy and excitement that it didn't matter what people thought of him.

Read

2 Samuel 6:12–22

Explain

David's first attempt to move the ark to Jerusalem had ended in disaster, but this time, he was much more careful. He moved the precious cargo in exactly the way God wanted, respecting and fearing His holiness. When the ark entered the city, David was so overcome with joy, gratitude, and excitement that he danced, and he danced without caring what other people thought. His wife, though, thought what David was doing was undignified. Surely a king should be more respectable than the display David was putting on! But David knew the opinions of those around him meant very little. What really mattered was what God thought, and God was pleased to have the ark dwell in Jerusalem.

We can learn a great deal from this because often, we hold ourselves back in our obedience to God because we are worried about what other people think. God, however, is calling us to a deep level of love and obedience for and to Him, regardless of what anyone else does.

Reflect

1. Why was David so excited?

2. How did he show his excitement?

3. What can we learn from what David did?

Pray

Lord, help us not to care so much about what other people think. Please let the most important thing in our lives be what You think.

Going up the Hill

Show

Ask each member of the family to wash their hands before coming to family devotion. When they get there, ask to inspect their hands, and then ask them if they are sure they're clean. Remind the family that we typically wash our hands after or before certain activities. Then tell them you just purchased a new device that you can shine on their hands that will tell you just how well they cleaned them. After asking them if anyone wants to try washing their hands again, reveal to them that you're just kidding about the device. Then transition and tell them that today you will read a song together that David wrote that mentions having clean hands. It's a song about a king, but not just any king—this is the King of Glory.

Read

Psalm 24

Explain

Perhaps David wrote this song to celebrate that the ark had come back to Jerusalem. Because the people believed God dwelled between the cherubim of the ark, it was a case of the King returning. The King of Glory—the Lord of Hosts—was coming to the capital city of Jerusalem. But David wasn't just interested in celebrating the return of the ark. He had an even more important question: Who can go up the hill and be in the presence of this King? It was only those with clean hands and a pure heart. Only those who are truly pure, both in heart and action, can come into the presence of God.

The only problem is that none of us can clean ourselves! Our hands will never truly be clean; our hearts will never truly be pure. We need a new heart, one without sin, in order to approach the Lord, and we can only find that through the King of Glory Himself.

Reflect

1. What are some of the ways David described the King of Glory?

2. Who is the King of Glory?

3. How can we approach this King?

Pray

Lord, You are indeed the King of Glory. Thank You that in Jesus, we can have clean hands and pure hearts.

An Enduring House

Show

Prior to family devotion, gather a bag of Legos, blocks, or other toy building materials. Present the items before the family, and tell them they will have two minutes to build a house that's as strong as possible with what you have given them. After two minutes have elapsed, congratulate the family on their work, and ask them to explain why they built the house the way they did. Comment again on how well they did, but then remind them that no matter how long they had, they would not be able to build a house from these materials that would last for very long. Transition to today's part of the story by explaining that God gave David a special promise—a covenant—that involved building houses. But the houses God talked about weren't like these houses, but something much more.

Read

2 Samuel 7:8–16

Explain

David had brought peace to the kingdom. The ark was in Jerusalem, David was in his palace, and no enemies were threatening. David decided he wanted to build a temple for the Lord.

But God had a surprising response to this, at least to David. God reminded David that He did not ask for a house from David; in fact, God wanted David to know that He, God, is the One who establishes who lives where, just as He had done with David and with all of Israel. Rather than David building a house for the Lord, the Lord would establish David's house. God made a covenant with David that his house—another way of saying his family—would have someone to sit on the throne for all eternity. Centuries later, Jesus would be born into David's family. And Jesus would be the eternal king, not sitting on a throne in Jerusalem, but sitting on a throne in heaven.

Reflect

1. What did David want to do for God?

2. What did God remind David of?

3. What did God promise to David?

Pray

Thank You, God, that You determine who the kings of earth are. Thank You that You have already established Jesus as the King over all.

The King and the Cripple

Show

Lead the family to brainstorm the following scenario. Let's say that today you received a letter in the mail inviting you to come to the home of a king or dignitary, and you had to be there tomorrow. Ask the family to brainstorm a "to-do list" of what you would need to accomplish and gather to have with you in order to be at dinner. Encourage the family to think about things like what they would need to wear, what customs they would need to learn about, and planning what they would say. Transition to today's part of the story by telling the family that this was, in a way, exactly what happened to a man named Mephibosheth, the son of Jonathan.

Read

2 Samuel 9:1–7

Explain

Mephibosheth must have thought life had passed him by. He was the son of Jonathan, who might well have been the future king of Israel. But when Saul and Jonathan died, everything went off the rails. In that day and time, when a new family took control of the throne, one of the first things the new ruler would do was to have everyone from the previous ruling family put to death so there would be no challenges to the throne. So, when word came that the king and his son were dead, Mephibosheth's nurse picked him up to flee, and in her haste, she dropped him. The fall was so bad that it crippled him in both feet. Then they ran to a new home where hopefully they could be safe.

David meanwhile set about the business of establishing himself as king. But David never forgot about his promise to Jonathan. He sent word looking for any relative of Saul and Jonathan—not so he could kill them, but so he could show kindness to them. Mephibosheth was brought to the palace. What an amazing sight it must have been between the king and the cripple! The ruler and the outcast. The rich and the poor. David, though he could have done anything he wanted, chose to bring Mephibosheth into his home and give him a place at his table. He did this not because the crippled young man had earned that place, but because of his father, Jonathan, and because of David's kindness. Like Mephibosheth, we are crippled spiritually, afflicted with sin. But God, the true King, has chosen to bring us into His home as His children. And He has done this not because we have earned it, but because of another—Jesus.

Reflect

1. Who was Mephibosheth?

2. What did David do for Mephibosheth?

3. How are we like Mephibosheth?

Pray

Lord, thank You that You are gracious and kind. Thank You that we can come into Your presence as Your children because of Jesus.

The King Falls

Show

For today's object lesson, bring to family devotion a piece of fresh food (cheese, slice of apple, etc.) and lay it before the family. Ask the family if they would be willing to eat it. Then explain that you are going to go put it under the couch, in a hidden place, and come back in two weeks. Ask if they would be willing to eat it then. As they react, ask them why not, and then point out that food like this spoils, and over time, it just gets worse and worse. Explain that in today's part of the story, we will read about how David sinned greatly, but rather than bringing that sin into the light immediately, he tried to cover it up. In its secrecy, the sin grew and compounded.

Read

2 Samuel 11:1–4

Explain

David should never have been on the roof to begin with. He should have been with his troops, but for whatever reason, David stayed at home, and while there he saw a beautiful woman who was not his wife. Rather than running from temptation as we saw Joseph do, David gave in and treated this woman like she was his wife and committed adultery with her. Again, David had the chance to repent of his sin, but instead of doing so he tried to cover it up. The woman became pregnant, and David knew the only way to cover up his sin was to take her as his wife. He arranged for her husband, a faithful soldier in David's army, to be killed so Bathsheba would be free to be married to someone else.

David, though he was a man after God's own heart and had done many great things for God, was not immune from temptation. David's sin shows us, among other things, that we are never really safe from sin. We must be on guard against it, trusting in God's strength, or we too will fall. But when we do, the worst thing we can do is try and cover it up.

Reflect

1. What should David have done after he sinned against Bathsheba, her husband, and God?

2. What did he do instead?

3. What does this part of David's life show us about ourselves?

Pray

Lord, please guard us from the pride that makes us think we cannot fall. Thank You that You will forgive us when we come to You, and please help us to come to You quickly after we sin.

The God Who Sees

Show

Bring a pile of pennies with you to family devotion. As you begin, give every penny except one to a member of the family. Then give the remaining penny to one other person. Then take the one penny and give it to the one who has the large pile of pennies, and ask the family to respond to this. What you have done was clearly not fair, taking the very little that one person had and giving it to the person who had very much. Transition to today's part of the story by explaining that David thought his sin and his attempts to cover it up had gone unnoticed. But God sees all, and He was about to let David know that.

Read

2 Samuel 12:1–13

Explain

God sees all. David must have thought that life had returned to normal; Bathsheba's husband was dead, and David had married her. Like Adam and Eve in the garden, David was trying to hide. But God revealed the truth to his prophet, Nathan, and the prophet confronted David with his sin using a story. The king was outraged at the thought that a man who already had so many sheep would take the single sheep belonging to someone else.

But David didn't realize that the story was really about him until Nathan revealed the truth.

God still sees all. Sometimes, we might sin in secret or just in our hearts and think no one knows, but God does. And like David, we have the choice about what to do when God brings our sin to light. We can either admit our wrongdoing and repent, or we can continue to hide. David made the right choice; the question is whether we will.

Reflect

1. How did God let David know He had seen David's sin?

2. What were David's choices when confronted by Nathan the prophet?

3. What should we do when we sin?

Pray

You are the God who sees all. Help us to know that we cannot hide anything from You, and help us to trust in Your mercy and grace and come to You for forgiveness.

Into the Light

Show

As family devotion begins, lead the family to a room which can be made very dark—maybe a basement or a large closet. Turn off all the lights, and tell the family that you will be having family devotion in that room today. Ask them to tell you why that might be a bad idea. Of course, it would be very difficult to read the Bible, see each other's faces, and talk to each other. Turn on the lights, and explain that in the Bible, light is always a good thing. Remind the family that David's sin had been brought from the darkness into the light, and after it was, David wrote the song you will read together today.

Read

Psalm 51

Explain

Psalm 51 is a song, but it's also a prayer. David knew he had sinned, and he was praying that God would restore him. David knew that he had no power to forgive his own sin, and no power to cleanse his heart. He asked God to do what only God can, which is to create in him a clean heart and restore his joy.

The good news of God's grace is that God can do the same thing for any of us. None of us are without sin, and none of us can do anything about it. But God can, and in His grace and mercy, He will. We can trust in God's grace and mercy, believing that in Jesus we can be saved from our sin and be given a new clean heart before God.

Reflect

1. What are some of the things David asked God to do?

2. What is the good news for us?

3. What does this psalm show us about the way we can approach God?

Pray

Thank You, God, that You are rich in mercy. Thank You that we can trust in Your grace and mercy to restore us and give us clean hearts.

Actions and Consequences

Show

Bring a ball with you to family devotion time. As the family gathers together, ask them what will happen if you throw the ball in the air. As they respond that the ball will fall to the ground, demonstrate the truth that it will indeed fall to the ground, then explain that this happens because of the natural law of gravity—what goes up must come down. This is somewhat similar to the way actions and consequences work. That is, there are consequences for actions we take. Transition to today's part of the story by telling the family that today we will see some of the consequences for David's actions.

Read

2 Samuel 12:15–23

Explain

David sinned with Bathsheba, covered up his sin, but then repented of his sin when Nathan the prophet confronted him. Though David received forgiveness and restoration from God, there were consequences for his actions. David earnestly prayed for the life of the child Bathsheba had given birth to, but one of the consequences for his actions was that the child died. This is a hard truth for us to accept, and we should be careful as we do. As we saw in the case of Job, this does not mean that every bad thing that happens in our lives is a consequence for something we have done. At the same time, we must recognize that forgiveness from God does not necessarily mean the removal of consequences for our actions.

There is a cost to sin, and many times it is the people around us who pay the price. Thankfully, the greatest cost for sin, which is death, has already been paid by Jesus. So even though we might bear the weight of the consequences of our sin, we never have to bear the weight of the ultimate consequence.

Reflect

1. What was one of the consequences for David's sin?

2. Is every bad thing that happens a consequence for something we have done wrong?

3. What is the ultimate consequence for sin?

Pray

Lord, help us to remember that our actions come with a cost, both to ourselves and others. Thank You for removing the greatest cost of our sin from us.

A Rebel Rises

Show

Explain to the family that you are going to play a game called "The Yes Game." The rules are simple—the family can ask you any question they want, and you will respond with a version of "yes." For example, they might ask to have cookies for breakfast, to which you would respond, "Absolutely." Remind them, of course, that it's only a game, and then play for a few minutes. As the game closes, ask them to think about whether they would like the game to be real. Ask them to consider what could potentially go wrong if the answer in life was always "yes." Then transition to today's portion of the story by telling the family that saying "Yes" to everything can make many people like you for a while, but it's a terrible way to lead a family, and as you will see today, a bad way to lead a nation as well.

Read

2 Samuel 15:1–6

Explain

As the story of David's life continues, we start to become acquainted with his children. One child in particular, Absalom, was very ambitious. In fact, Absalom began to plan to take the throne from his father, David. His plan was very shrewd—rather than challenging David outright for power, he began to intercept people who were seeking to meet with David, telling them that the king was too busy to hear their problems and issues. He flattered them, made promises to them, and planted the seed in their minds that if he were king instead of David, he would say "yes" to anything they desired. Slowly but surely, the hearts of the people left David and moved toward Absalom, which paved the way for an outright rebellion. Soon David would find himself on the run again, this time not from Saul but from his own son.

Our hearts are very fickle—they can change directions easily. We are, in many ways, like the people of Israel who wanted a king besides God; though we have a true King in Jesus, we can easily be lured away to trust in another who seems to give us more of what we want. We must remind our own hearts that God knows what's best for us, and even when His answer to what we want is no, He still loves us and will give us what we need.

Reflect

1. Who was Absalom?

2. How did Absalom create a rebellion in the kingdom?

3. How are we like the people of Israel?

Pray

Our hearts are prone to wander from You, Lord. Help us to remain steadfast in our faith, trusting in Your love and wisdom.

The Rebel Falls

Show

Explain to the family that in the same way you played the "Yes" game yesterday, today you will play the "No" game. You, as the parent, will ask the children a series of questions. Their job is to say "No" to everything you ask. After you go through a series of creative questions, stop the game and then ask the family to reflect on what would happen if the kids suddenly decided to say "no" to everything their parents told them to do. There would, of course, be consequences. This would be an act of rebellion in the home. As you continue the story today, you'll see that there were also consequences for Absalom's rebellion against his own father.

Read

2 Samuel 18:28–33

Explain

The rebellion was over, and the rebel was dead. David's kingdom had been restored, but it had come at a heavy price. Not only were many people killed in the rebellion, David's own son was dead as a consequence of his actions.

While we might expect David to feel a sense of relief at having won the battle for the kingdom, he did not. Instead, David felt overwhelming grief at the loss of his son, even though his son was a rebel who had sought to replace him as king.

See, not only are we like the Israelites who so easily shifted their loyalty; we are also like Absalom who rebelled against his father who loved him. All our sin is an act of rebellion against our true Father and King who loves us. When we sin, we are saying to God that we would be a better king over our lives than He is. And yet God does not rejoice when sinners receive what they deserve; He does not rejoice at the death of rebels. God desires not to put down our rebellion, but instead for rebels to see the error of their ways and return to Him as His children.

Reflect

1. What happened to Absalom, and how did David respond?

2. How do we see ourselves in Absalom?

3. How does David remind us of God?

Pray

Thank You, Father, that You do not rejoice in the death of rebels. Thank You, instead, that You love us even though we are sinners and rebels.

Last Words

Show

Explain to the family that today's part of the story involves the last recorded words of King David. Before examining those words, read some other last words of famous people through history:

- Italian artist Raphael's last word was simply: "Happy."
- When Harriet Tubman was dying in 1913, she gathered her family around and they sang together. Her last words were, "Swing low, sweet chariot."
- As Benjamin Franklin lay dying at the age of eighty-four, his daughter told him to change position in bed so he could breathe more easily. Franklin's last words were, "A dying man can do nothing easy."

Emphasize to the family that someone's last words can be really important. If a person knows they are going to die, then they will likely try to communicate something important about their lives and what matters to them. That's exactly what we see in the case of King David.

Read

2 Samuel 23:1–7

Explain

David lived a long life. He had come from the humble beginnings of a shepherd boy, been in the court of the king, won miraculous battles, and then faithfully served God and the people as king. He also knew what it meant to fail as a father, leader, and king. But now, as he knew he was close to death, David's last words were not filled with his own accomplishments or his regrets. Instead, his words were focused on God. David knew that the reason he was able to do anything with his life was because the Lord was with him. And, as he wrote in Psalm 23, he knew that even in the valley of the shadow of death, the Lord would still preserve him.

If we are the children of God, having been rescued from our sin, then even as our lives come to an end, we can still count on Him to be faithful to us.

Reflect

1. What sticks out to you from David's last words?

2. How did David show gratitude to God?

3. What do we learn about God's faithfulness from David's life and death?

Pray

Thank You, God, that You will be faithful to us even to the end. Help us to not lose faith even during dark days.

A Wise Request

Show

Bring a sponge with you to family devotion. Soak the sponge until it's saturated, then explain to the family that the sponge is meant to show us what wisdom is, and what it is not. Explain that sometimes we think wisdom is like this sponge, soaking in knowledge. But soaking in knowledge is not the same thing as wisdom. Real wisdom is not gathering in knowledge, but it's using what we know in real practical ways. Knowledge doesn't become wisdom until it's wrung out and used.

Read

1 Kings 3:1–10

Explain

King David was dead, and his son, Solomon, would take the throne. God came to Solomon and gave him an incredible gift—the Lord told Solomon that He would give Solomon whatever he asked for. Imagine all the things the new king might have requested from the true King of the universe! He could have asked for wealth, for power, for long life; but instead, Solomon made the wisest request of all. He knew that in order to lead the nation, the thing he needed more than anything else was wisdom, and that's what he asked God for. God was pleased with

Solomon's humble request, and he gave him what he asked for. Soon Solomon would be known all over the world for his wisdom.

We, too, should be humble enough to know what we truly need. To live a life honoring to God and join Him on His mission, we need wisdom that only God can provide.

Reflect

1. What did Solomon ask from God?

2. Why was God pleased with Solomon's request?

3. What is the difference between wisdom and knowledge?

Pray

Give us, Lord, what only You can give. Give us true wisdom so that we might live for You.

Like a Tree

Show

Guide the family outside and sit together under a tree for today's family devotion. Ask the family to consider the tree. Ask them to feel the bark, look at the limbs, and observe as much about it as they can. Then ask them to try and push the tree over, and when they can't, ask them why not. Explain that the tree gets its strength from its roots. The deeper the roots go down, the stronger the tree is. Transition to today's part of the story by telling the family that you will read a psalm that has a tree in it. And like the tree you are under, the one in the psalm finds its strength from its roots.

Read

Psalm 1

Explain

Psalm 1 represents two different kinds of people. As we saw with Solomon, God wants His children to live in wisdom, and that's the first kind of person. This person is blessed, or happy, according to the psalm. They are as strong as a tree because their roots run deep. They find their wisdom in the Word of God, which reveals to them the way in which they are meant to live. The second type of person is the fool. Unlike the wise person, this person does not have deep roots, and so they blow away when troubles come their way.

In the end, we can know that the Lord watches over the way of those who are humbly committed to him. And for the wicked? It's just a matter of time until their ways catch up to them.

Reflect

1. What are we meant to learn from the image of the tree in Psalm 1?

2. What separates the righteous and the wicked in this psalm?

3. How can we make sure our roots run deep?

Pray

Lord, You have shown us the pathway of life. Help us to live according to Your Word so our roots might run deep.

Under Construction

Show

Bring a common set of household tools with you to family devotion time. Present the tools before the family, and ask them for some things they think you could build together as a family using those tools. Then ask them for a list of things you would not be able to build together using those tools. Transition to today's part of the story by telling them that the time had come for another construction project. This one would be greater than the construction of the ark, greater than the construction of the tabernacle. The time had come to build the temple of the Lord.

Read

1 Kings 5:1–6

Explain

David wanted to build a temple for the Lord, a place where the people could worship and God's presence would reside. But God let David know that this task was not for him to do, but instead, for the new king, Solomon. So Solomon set about planning for the massive project that would involve far more than common, household tools. He employed a work force that would number 30,000, began importing timber from other lands, and intricately designed both the interior and exterior. The temple would be a sight to behold indeed. But more than its beauty, the temple would serve as yet another reminder that God desires not to be far from His people, but instead to live closely with them, just as He does today.

Reflect

1. Why did Solomon want to build the temple?

2. Why was the temple important?

3. What does the temple show us about the heart of God?

Pray

Thank You, God, that You do not desire distance from us. Help us to desire to be with You like You want to be near us.

The Temple Filled

Show

As you gather for family devotion, ask the family to make a brief list of things you would need to have on hand for a special birthday party. They might list things like hats, cake, streamers, and other decorations. After they have had a chance to make the list, affirm their choices, but then remind them that most everything on the list is really just to create the environment for the party. The most important element of any birthday party is the person being celebrated. Without him or her, all the decorations really don't matter. Similarly, today you will read what happens next in our story as Solomon and his workers prepared the temple. Now they needed the most important part.

Read

1 Kings 8:3–11

Explain

Everything was ready. An extreme amount of time, money, and effort had gone into building the temple, and everything was just right. But none of the elaborate decoration or intricate detail could match what happened next. As the people gathered to dedicate the temple to the Lord, the presence of the Lord came down in a cloud. Just as happened hundreds of years earlier in the wilderness. God made His presence known again and He filled the innermost part of the temple. The priests could not even continue their work because of the presence of the Lord. What an amazing day it must have been! Solomon's desire, as he would pray, was that the temple be a place where people from all over the world could come and meet with the one, true God.

Now as we keep reading the story, we will see that as beautiful as the temple was, it would not last. It would eventually be destroyed, but God's desire to live closely with His people would not. In fact, a day would come when the Lord would be even closer than the city of Jerusalem. He would set up His temple in the very hearts of His people.

Reflect

1. What was the most important part of the temple?

2. What do you think it looked like when the Lord's presence filled the temple?

3. What did Solomon desire the temple to be?

Pray

Thank You again, Lord, that You desire to live with Your people. Thank You that in Christ, You actually make Your temple in our hearts.

Wealth and Wisdom

Show

Bring a $1 bill, a debit or credit card, and a blank check with you to family devotion and show them to the family. Ask them what all these things have in common? Explain that today, these are the forms of money we use, but in Solomon's day, wealth would have looked very different. Instead of paper money, wealth was measured in things like gold, and Solomon had a lot of it. The Bible says that Solomon took in 25 tons of gold a year, and 1 ton of gold is worth about $47 million. That happened every year!

Read

1 Kings 10:23–25

Explain

Solomon's wealth and wisdom were unsurpassed in the ancient world. The Bible tells us of his golden shields, his throne made of ivory, and all his dishes that were made of pure gold. Not only was he wealthy, but God was faithful to increase Solomon's wisdom. He was so wise that other leaders from all over the world traveled to Israel just to spend time with him and learn from him. Solomon studied all different kinds of things in his lifetime. He was educated, powerful, wise, and rich beyond measure. He had, in other words, everything.

And yet in the midst of all his great blessings, Solomon was not wise enough to avoid temptation. Solomon would not remain faithful to the Lord, and in this, we see the truth that prosperity can often make us forget our reliance on God. We can often forget the source of our blessings and turn again and again to false gods just as we will see Solomon doing.

Reflect

1. How wealthy was Solomon?

2. How wise was Solomon?

3. What was the danger in his prosperity?

Pray

Lord, You have been good to us in so many ways. Please guard us from the temptation to forget about the source of all the blessings in our lives.

A Drifting Heart

Show

Ask for a volunteer from the family, and then ask the person to stand up. Hand them a piece of fruit like an apple and ask them how heavy it is. Of course, it will be very light. But then ask them to extend their arm straight out in front of them holding the fruit and keep it straight without falling. As the volunteer stands there, start a conversation with the rest of the family, asking them about their day, what they plan to do, etc. At the same time, keep an eye on the person with the fruit, and gradually their arm will begin to drop. As it does, remark that their arm is moving, and remind them they said the fruit was light. Use this as a transition to explain that even the strongest person cannot hold their arm out straight forever; it will eventually fall. Sometimes it happens so slowly that you don't even realize it's happening. Explain that this is the way sin happens in our hearts many times. If we aren't careful, our hearts slowly start to slip away from God; sometimes it happens so gradually we don't even know it has happened until it's already done. This is what we will see today in the life of Solomon.

Read

1 Kings 11:1–6

Explain

Solomon had every blessing imaginable—wealth, power, wisdom, and prosperity. But in all his luxury, his heart began to drift from God. The same king who built the temple and witnessed the glory of the Lord fill it slowly but surely drifted from the Lord. The Lord had warned His people how dangerous it was to marry people who worshiped other gods because God knew it would result in idolatry. Perhaps Solomon thought himself strong enough to avoid temptation; perhaps he thought his life was secure because of his wealth and power. But he was neither strong enough nor secure enough. His heart was easily swayed.

Like Solomon, our hearts are easily swayed. And despite having all the privilege in the world, he departed from the Lord and worshiped false gods. Like Samson before him, Solomon was not faithful.

Reflect

1. Why do you think Solomon started worshiping other gods?

2. Is that surprising to you? Why or why not?

3. What does this teach us about our own hearts?

Pray

Help us, Lord, to guard our hearts. Help us to remember our weakness and trust in Your strength to make us faithful people.

Futile!

Show

Bring a wrapped empty package with you to family devotion. Show the package to everyone, and ask them to imagine and guess what's inside based on the wrapping paper. Then unwrap the package and show them that it's actually empty. Explain that in a way, the outside of the box lied to them. It promised to have something valuable inside, but in the end, there was really nothing. Explain that today you will look at one of the books of the Bible that Solomon wrote—the book of Ecclesiastes. And Solomon, in all his wisdom, came to the same conclusion you came to when looking at the box.

Read

Ecclesiastes 1:1–11

Explain

"Futility!" This one word occurs over and over again in the book of Ecclesiastes. Solomon made a study of everything under the sun. He studied wisdom, philosophy, time, pleasure, science, and anything else he could find. In all these subjects, Solomon plumbed the depths, learning as much as he could, each time thinking that the subject might give meaning to his life. But in the end, every one of these things was like a beautifully wrapped but empty package. They promised great things, but when he got to the bottom of them, he found they were empty.

Life is like that—we can immerse ourselves in any number of things. We might spend our lives going after money, or power, or a good job, or a family, but without God, life is futile and without meaning. In the end, the wisest thing Solomon ever said was that life is actually very simple. Meaning is not found in any other pursuit except knowing and obeying God. We can only find a life that's meaningful when we fear God and keep His commands.

Reflect

1. What's the one word that appears over and over in the book of Ecclesiastes?

2. Why did Solomon use that word?

3. What does this book teach us about life?

Pray

Thank You, Lord, that You alone can give us a life of meaning. Help us to find our meaning in You rather than wasting our time looking for it in other places and things.

Fear the Lord

Show

As the family gathers together, take out a match and light it, allowing it to burn for a few seconds. Then ask the family to tell you some of the rules people should follow when they are working with fire of any kind. After a few examples, ask them another question: Should fire be feared? This is a more complicated question, because the answer is yes and no. Fire should be feared because it can be dangerous, but it's also something we really need to live. So the fear of fire should be a healthy respect and caution because we know what it's capable of. Use this illustration to move the family further into the devotion, asking them to keep that in mind as you read from the Bible today.

Read

Proverbs 1:1–7

Explain

Solomon, in addition to all his pursuits, was committed to writing down the wisdom he had obtained for the benefit of others. Many of the proverbs we have in the Bible were written by Solomon, and they are there for our benefit. It's important to remember that proverbs are not promises; rather, they are descriptions of how the world generally works and a general description of the way we are to operate in life. In Proverbs 1, Solomon began by telling us all the benefits of wisdom. But then he reminded us that the beginning of wisdom is not knowledge; it's the fear of the Lord.

But fearing the Lord is not the same thing as being afraid of the Lord. For those that are in a right relationship with God through Jesus, fearing the Lord means having a healthy respect for Him and devotion to Him. Like the way we treat fire, we should have a reverence for God, remembering that He is the Ruler of the universe. When we live our lives in holy reverence for God and His power, we will begin to live in wisdom.

Reflect

1. What is the beginning of wisdom?

2. What does it mean to fear the Lord?

3. What are some of the ways we show that we fear the Lord?

Pray

Help us, God, not to become too comfortable and casual with You. Help us to remember who You are, and live in the fear of the Lord.

Seek Wisdom

Show

Prior to family devotion, take a bowl and fill it with sand. Then place a coin in the sand and cover it up. Present the bowl of sand to the family and ask for a volunteer to see how long it takes them to find the coin hidden in it. Time the family member, then ask for another volunteer to play the same game and see who wins. Explain that the coin was there for both people; both people, though, had to actually seek it out. Explain that as we read another of Solomon's set of proverbs, we will see that this is similar to the way he described wisdom.

Read

Proverbs 2:1–9

Explain

Wisdom is precious. Solomon makes that clear. But wisdom is also available for those who want to put in the time and effort to obtain it. According to Solomon, true wisdom begins with the fear of the Lord, but both must be sought after. So how do we seek after wisdom? How do we dig it out, like a treasure hidden in the sand? Solomon gives us the key. We must know, love, and obey the Word of God, and as we do, the process is like digging in the sand. Slowly but surely, we will find the wisdom that is available to us.

Centuries later, the book of James tells us that we should also diligently ask God for wisdom because He is willing to give it to us generously. Ask God for wisdom. Read His Word. Obey it. As you do, over the course of time you actually become a wise person as God's Word shapes the way you think about everything. This is how we learn to fear the Lord and become wise people.

Reflect

1. What are the ways that we find wisdom?

2. What are some of the things God has told us to do in His Word?

3. What are some ways we can make sure, as a family, we are obeying God's Word?

Pray

God, You have told us to ask You for wisdom because You are willing to give it. We want to obey You, so we ask You to make our family a wise family who obeys Your Word.

Trust, Not Understanding

Show

As you begin family devotion, walk over to a light switch in the room. Ask the family what will happen if you flip the switch, and allow them to respond. But then ask them *why* that would happen—why specifically would the light go on and off when you flip the switch? Explain that in a sense, you are trusting that the light switch will operate the light. You don't have to understand all the ways in which the circuits, light bulbs, and electricity work together in order to believe it's going to happen. Further explain that a person can still trust even when they don't understand. Point the family to today's Bible passage, explaining that in the proverbs you will read today, you'll see that there is a difference between trusting and understanding.

Read

Proverbs 3:1–7

Explain

Living a life pleasing to God is fundamentally about trust. In this passage, we see the command to trust in the Lord with all our hearts. But we also see what we might be tempted to do instead of trusting in the Lord—that is, we might try to lean on our own understanding. This is a dangerous way to live because when we trust ourselves and our understanding more than trusting God, we are putting ourselves in God's place. God wants us to trust Him, and to show that trust by obeying Him, even when His commands might not make sense to us, might lead us into difficulty, or when our circumstances might be painful. Of course, that doesn't mean we don't use our minds to think clearly about decisions we have to make. It does mean, though, that we must primarily use our faith, and let our faith inform the way we are thinking. When we trust instead of leaning on our own understanding, we show that we truly believe God is good, generous, and wise.

Reflect

1. What might we do instead of trust God?

2. Why is it difficult to trust God when you don't understand what He's doing or commanding you to do?

3. What do we show about our beliefs when we lean on our own understanding instead of trusting God?

Pray

Lord, You alone know the pathway of life. Help us to trust in You with all our hearts and follow wherever You lead.

Torn in Two

Show

On a sheet of paper, write the word "Israel." Remind the family that the Israelites had become a nation under their first king, Saul, but they had always been one people even back to the days of their father, Abraham. Now take the paper and tear it in half, and write "Israel" on one side and "Judah" on the other. Further explain that something new was about to happen in the land, and it came as a consequence of disobedience.

Read

1 Kings 11:9–13

Explain

Actions have consequences. Sin has consequences. And though Solomon was wise beyond anyone else, wealthy beyond all imagination, and prosperous nearly beyond belief, he was lulled to sleep in his heart. Solomon abandoned the Lord to worship other gods, and there would be consequences for it. God would tear the kingdom of Israel in half. Soon after the death of Solomon, the kingdom was divided between Solomon's son, Rehoboam and one of Solomon's own servants, Jeroboam. After a long period of peace and prosperity under David and then Solomon, so began the slow decline of both the nations of Israel and Judah into idolatry. And though the people might have thought, like Solomon, that there were no consequences for their disobedience, eventually God would judge both nations for their sin.

We must never mistake the patience of God for an uncaring posture. In His mercy, God allows us time to repent of our sin and turn to Him for forgiveness and rescue, but His patience will not last forever.

Reflect

1. Why did God tear the kingdom in two?

2. What were the two new nations called?

3. What can we learn about God's patience and judgment from this?

Pray

Lord, forgive us for mistaking Your mercy and patience for You not caring. Help us to see the urgency of turning from our sin to You for forgiveness.

Flour and Oil

Show

Place a box of tissues in front of the family as you begin family devotion. Ask them what will happen if you pull a tissue out of the box. Obviously, another tissue will come up in its place. Explain that you might do this many more times, and a tissue will still come up. But eventually, you will come to the last tissue in the box, and then there won't be anything left to replace it. In order for the tissues to go on appearing forever, there would have to be an inexhaustible supply of tissues feeding into the box. Now transition to today's portion of the story, explaining that you will see today that God's resources have no limit. He can provide for all His children, for all time.

Read

1 Kings 17:8–16

Explain

The kingdom of Israel was split into two kingdoms—Israel in the north, and Judah in the south. Eventually, a wicked king named Ahab rose to the throne in the north, but the true power, and the even greater wickedness, did not lie with Ahab but instead to his wife, Jezebel. Elijah was the prophet of God who stood against the idolatry and evil of the king and queen, and they hated him for it. Elijah, though, remained committed to following the Word of the Lord, so when God told him to go to a place called Zarephath, he got up and went.

God knows everything and everyone, and cares for even the least among all humanity, so it should not surprise us that God was willing to send someone as seemingly important as Elijah to help someone as seemingly unimportant as this nameless widow. Her situation was desperate, and God saw her need. He provided for her in a miraculous way. She would not go hungry; just as God provided manna for the Israelites in the wilderness every morning, so also would this woman find each day that she had everything she needed to make bread.

No matter how small we think we are, God sees us. And not only does He see us, He will provide all we need from His abundant riches.

Reflect

1. How did God provide for the widow?

2. What can we learn from this part of the story about God?

3. What is the difference in God giving us everything we want and everything we need?

Pray

Lord, thank You that there is no one too small for You. Thank You that we can trust You to care for us and provide what we need.

The Challenger

Show

Gather a bowl full of water and a book of matches. Show the family the bowl of water, then light a match over it and drop it into the bowl. Repeat this same thing again and again, commenting that the natural way of things is for water to extinguish fire, not the other way around. But as we will see in today's part of the story, God is not limited by the usual way of things.

Read

1 Kings 18:20–24

Explain

A line was being drawn in the sand. It was time for the people to decide who they would worship—would it be the idols that Ahab and Jezebel clung to, or would it be the one true God of Elijah? Elijah proposed a simple challenge. Both he and the prophets of Baal would set up an altar, both would pray to their god, and the true God would answer the prayer and consume the sacrifice with fire. All day long the prophets of Baal chanted. And prayed. And shouted. And even harmed themselves believing if they were only loud enough they could get the attention of Baal, their god. But Elijah knew the truth: Baal was no god at all. So when it came time for Elijah to pray, he not only laid the sacrifice on the alter but also dug a trench around the altar and filled it with water. Then he prayed a simple but bold prayer, and the Lord answered. Fire fell from above and consumed not only the offering, but the whole altar and all the water around it. There was no doubt who the winner of the challenge was, and there was no doubt who was the true God.

Like Elijah, we can be confident in God. We can pray simple but bold prayers, trusting the Lord will answer them. And like Elijah, we can stand firmly in the truth even when we are standing alone.

Reflect

1. What was the challenge Elijah laid out?

2. How did God meet the challenge?

3. How can this story encourage us in our faith today?

Pray

You alone are God—there is no one like You. Help us to truly believe that, and to not be afraid to pray boldly to You.

The Still, Small Voice

Show

Challenge the family as you sit down for family devotion to be as quiet as they can for thirty seconds. And as you are being quiet, challenge them to really listen. After thirty seconds, ask everyone to comment on what they were able to hear when they were quiet. Perhaps they were able to hear the buzz of a refrigerator, the traffic outside, or the ticking of a clock. These were things that were always in the background, but until the family was very quiet no one was able to really take notice of them. Transition to today's part of the story by telling the family that today you will read about a time when Elijah heard the voice of the Lord, but His voice didn't sound like what you might expect.

Read

1 Kings 19:9–13

Explain

Even though God had responded to Elijah's challenge to the prophets of Baal, Ahab and Jezebel were increasingly angry with him and threatened to kill him. Elijah ran for his life and took shelter in a cave. That's when the word of the Lord came to him, and Elijah went out on the mountain to stand in God's presence. That's when all the noise started. An earthquake, a mighty wind, and even a fire swept through, and they were all big, noisy things. But it was not until the noise died down that Elijah heard God's voice in the quiet like a whisper.

We might expect God to speak in big, noisy ways, but it's only when our minds and hearts are quiet that we can really take in the Word of God. God is speaking to us through His Word all the time—the only question is whether or not we are quiet enough to listen.

Reflect

1. Why was Elijah in the cave?

2. How did God speak to Elijah?

3. How does God speak to us today?

Pray

Lord, we live in a noisy world. Please help us to be quiet enough in our hearts and minds to listen to You.

In the Whirlwind

Show

Present the family with a few patterns of numbers, seeing if they can find the pattern and guess the next number in the sequence. For example, what is the next number in this pattern: 1, 4, 9, 16 ? The answer is 25, since each number in the sequence is a number squared. Explain that in these cases there is a definite sequence. Likewise, there is a definite sequence in life, and it's the same for everyone: We are born, we live, we die. But explain that when we come to the end of Elijah's story, we see this pattern is broken.

Read

2 Kings 2:8–12

Explain

Elijah lived a remarkable life of obedience and power. As the prophet of the Lord, He stood in the face of evil and spoke truth, but now it was time for the Lord to raise up and empower a new prophet, Elisha. Elisha was humble enough to know that he could do nothing on his own; like Elijah, he would need the power of the Lord if he was to be God's prophet, and he would have it. But in one last display of power, the Lord broke the pattern of birth, life, and death, for Elijah did not actually die, but was instead taken from earth up into heaven. Can you imagine it? God's prophet taken in a flaming chariot up to be with his Lord. But while this prophet was taken up, the time was getting closer and closer to when God Himself would come down, not in a chariot, but in the form of a baby.

Reflect

1. What did Elisha ask for?

2. Why was this a good request?

3. What happened to Elijah?

Pray

Lord, help us to remember what Elisha knew, that apart from You we can do nothing.

The Mantle Passes

Show

Prior to family devotion, look through the closets in your home to see if you can find any "hand-me-down" clothes, or clothing that belonged to one member of the family and now belongs to a different member. Gather a few pieces of clothing like this and bring them with you, then ask the family to identify who the owner is of each piece of clothing. Explain that this might be a difficult question, because the clothing has been worn by multiple people, passed from one to another. Transition to today's part of the story, explaining that in this story, too, we will see a piece of hand-me-down clothing, but in this case, the clothing represented something far greater than the person who owns it.

Read

2 Kings 2:12–15

Explain

Elijah had gone up to heaven, but he had left behind a piece of clothing. His mantle, which was a kind of cloak, had fallen off, and this was a sign to Elisha. Elisha had asked for a double share of the spirit of Elijah, knowing he would need the power and presence of God if he were to be the next prophet. As a symbol of this transition, the mantle was left behind and then passed to Elisha who put it on.

Like Elisha, we need a different spirit in us if we are to accomplish anything worthwhile for God. Thankfully, the Holy Spirit lives in us when we believe in Jesus. And God does not withhold any of His Spirit; we have total access to God's Spirit. For us, then, the question is not whether we have the Spirit within us; it's whether we are going to surrender to the influence of the Spirit in our lives.

Reflect

1. What symbolized the transition from Elijah to Elisha?

2. What spirit do we need to accomplish work for God?

3. What do you think it means to surrender to the work of the Holy Spirit?

Pray

Help us, Lord, not to hold anything back from You but instead to fully surrender ourselves to the work of the Holy Spirit.

A Son Raised

Show

Gather together a Sharpie or marker, a piece of paper, and an eraser for family devotion. Using the marker, draw a long line on a piece of paper. Then hand the paper and the eraser to a member of the family and ask them to erase it. When it can't be done, remark that you have given them an impossible task. In fact, the family member might well have told you that erasing that line was impossible. Remark that it is indeed impossible, and that for us, as humans, many things are impossible. But there is nothing impossible with God, as you will see in the next part of the story.

Read

2 Kings 4:27–37

Explain

It was a miracle that this woman had a son to begin with. Like Abraham and Sarah of years gone by, this woman and her husband were also childless, and were now too old to bear children. This woman, though, was kind, generous, and hospitable to Elisha, always making room for him in her home when he passed by, and God took notice. And, as he had done for Sarah and Abraham, He gave her the miraculous gift of a son. But this great gift of God looked as though it had been taken away, for the son became ill and died. With God, though, there is no such thing as a lost cause. In a seemingly strange way, God used Elisha to raise the son from the dead.

In this miracle, we see a reminder of God's power and His faithfulness. God is a God of resurrection. Of new life. That is precisely what He does in us when we trust in Him for forgiveness—He raises us from spiritual death to spiritual life. And that can happen to anyone, regardless of who they are or where they come from.

Reflect

1. How is this woman like Sarah?

2. What miracles did God perform in the woman's life?

3. What does this part of the story remind us of about God?

Pray

You are the God who has power over life and death. Help us to remember that there is no such thing as a lost cause with You.

The Proud Warrior

Show

Present before the family two bowls of water. Then take a cup full of dirt and mix it in one of the bowls. Then ask the family which one they would prefer to use to wash their hands and why. Transition to the next part of the story by explaining that one of the lessons we need to consistently learn in this story is that you can't always trust your eyes. You have to live by faith. Explain that today you will meet a proud warrior who needed to get his skin clean, but he was having trouble believing it could be done.

Read

2 Kings 5:9–15

Explain

Namaan was a great warrior in a foreign land, but he had a servant girl who was an Israelite. Despite all his power in battle, Namaan was powerless to heal himself from the skin disease of leprosy. But his servant knew a way—she knew of Elisha, and she knew that God worked through him. The servant girl told her master, and Namaan made his way to seek out the prophet. But when he got there, he was surprised to find that Elisha didn't even come out to meet him. Not only that, but he sent a message that Namaan should dunk himself in a dirty river. Namaan was insulted; after all, he was a very important commander. It seems that Namaan's heart was as sick as his skin. But at the urging of his servants, he did as Elisha said and washed himself in the Jordan. And guess what—he was healed.

We must be careful when we come to God that we don't think ourselves too important to do what He tells us to do. Instead, we must come to Him in faith, trusting that whatever He tells us is the right thing.

Reflect

1. What was Namaan's problem?

2. Was Namaan's real problem with his skin, or with something else?

3. What lesson do you think Namaan learned from this?

Pray

Lord, we are prideful people. Help us to humble ourselves before You, and to show that humility by doing exactly what You say.

For Us

Show

Walk the family outside and encourage everyone to look upward, and ask them what is up there. They will likely respond with things like clouds, birds, and trees, but encourage them to think about things that are there, and yet not visible. Some example might be high-flying airplanes, oxygen, other elements, and all kinds of radio waves. The point of the exercise is to see that there is far more happening than what is visible. Explain that this is also true spiritually, and it's a lesson Elisha helped his servant, Gehazi, learn.

Read

2 Kings 6:8–17

Explain

The king of Aram was waging war against Israel, but it was a frustrating experience. Every time the king tried to ambush the Israelites, they always seemed to know what was coming. The king was convinced that there must be a spy in his court, for that was the only way the Israelites could know this information. But one of his servants let him know that there was no spy; instead, Elisha was a prophet who heard straight from God. The king knew that if he could kill Elisha, then the victory could be his, so he focused his efforts on finding the prophet and sent an army to surround the village where he was staying. Gehazi, the servant of Elisha, was terrified when he saw the army, but Elisha knew something Gehazi didn't—that you cannot always trust your eyes. Elisha knew that God's own army was protecting them, and that army was far greater and more powerful than the one from Aram.

What a wonderful thing to know that we do not have to trust our eyes only, and God is not only with us but for us. We must choose to live by faith, trusting that when our purposes are aligned with God's, His resources will always be available for us.

Reflect

1. How were the Israelites able to continually defeat the king of Aram?

2. What lesson did Elisha teach Gehazi, and how?

3. Why is it important for us to know that God is not only with us, but for us?

Pray

Thank You, Lord, that Your resources and power never run out. Help us to live by faith and not by sight.

The Kingdom Falls

Show

Walk the family outside for a water relay race to begin devotion time. Place two large bowls about twenty feet apart. One of the bowls should be larger than the other, and fill the larger bowl with water. Then give each family member a small paper cup. Explain that you will see how fast the family, one member and one cup at a time, can fill the smaller bowl with the larger bowl. Start the race and make note of the time it takes to make the smaller bowl overflow. If you have time, you might repeat the race a few times to see if you can improve the time. Then transition to the next part of the story, explaining that over the years the northern kingdom of Israel had a string of kings that led the people further and further into idolatry. With each passing year, judgment was being stored up for the people, just as the smaller bowl was being filled up with water.

Read

2 Kings 17:6–18

Explain

Judgment had been a long time in coming. God had warned the people hundreds of years earlier to be careful about coming into the new land, but His warnings had gone unheeded. Though there had been a few bright spots, God's people consistently fell into patterns of idolatry. Eventually, the idolatry became so accepted and obvious in the land that there were statues and idols set up all over. God, in His mercy, gave the people chance after chance to repent. He sent prophet after prophet to deliver warnings and pleadings for them to return to Him, but the people chose to go their own way.

God's mercy will not last forever; it wouldn't for the Israelites and it won't for us. Today, idolatry still exists. It's true we might not have statues set up in our homes, but we tend to worship other things than God. We worship money, power, safety, and comfort, and God pleads with us in His Word to worship Him alone. In His mercy, God continues to offer us a way to come back to Him—through believing in Jesus and following Him alone, but we should be careful to realize that we only have one life, and God's mercy will not last forever.

Reflect

1. Why did the northern kingdom of Israel fall?

2. How did God show His mercy to the people?

3. What can we learn about God's mercy and His judgment from this part of the story?

Pray

Lord, help us not to put off until tomorrow what should be done today. Help us to come to Jesus rather than waiting, and to tell others to do the same thing.

A King Is Healed

Show

Walk the family outside and ask for a volunteer to stand in the sun. As they do, go behind them and trace their shadow with chalk. Then ask them to consider what would happen to the shadow if they stood there all day long. As the day went on, the shadow would eventually become longer. This is the natural way of things. But in the next part of the story, we will see something miraculous happening—the shadow of the king would not get longer, but instead get shorter.

Read

2 Kings 20:1–10

Explain

As idolatry and judgment were sweeping the northern kingdom of Israel, the southern kingdom of Judah was being led by King Hezekiah, a king who loved and worshiped God. God's prophet, Isaiah, faithfully spoke the Word of God to the king and the people, and Hezekiah was willing to listen. But the king became terribly ill, and when he did, he did just the right thing—he turned to the Lord for help. In His grace, God even provided Hezekiah with a miraculous sign that he would be

228

healed. His shadow would go backward, a miraculous display of God's power.

God is faithful to those who turn to Him. When we come to God in humility, we can rest knowing that He hears our prayers. And though we should not expect to always have the same response God gave to Hezekiah, we should always expect God to meet His children with compassion, wisdom, and grace.

Reflect

1. What was Hezekiah's problem, and what did he do about it?

2. How did God respond?

3. How does this encourage us in our prayers?

Pray

Thank You, God, that You are attentive to the needs of Your children. Help us to always come to You quickly and humbly in prayer when we are in need.

The Suffering Servant

Show

    The object lesson for the next part of the story is a telescope. If you have a telescope in the house, bring it with you to family devotion. If not, pull up a picture of one online to show the family. Explain that telescopes are remarkable things. The most powerful ones can be shot into orbit and can see millions of miles away, giving us information about the universe. But no matter how powerful a telescope is, it cannot see into the future. Only God can do that. But occasionally, God gave His people a picture of what was to come through His prophets. This is what He did with the prophet Isaiah, and Isaiah 53 is a lens through which God's people could see the Savior He would send to them. But the picture they saw was something unexpected.

Read

Isaiah 53:1–12

Explain

    Isaiah gave the people the clearest picture yet of the Messiah, or Savior, who was to come. The problem was—and still is—that this Savior was unexpected. He would not have the look of a Savior. And He would not act like the kind of hero the people wanted. He was not a conquering war hero or a political leader;

He would instead be a servant who would die on behalf of the people He loves. Though this was not the kind of Savior the people wanted, it was the only Savior they really needed.

So it is with us. We must accept Jesus, the Savior who was to come, and who has come, as He is, and as the Bible describes Him. We don't get to tell God what kind of Savior we want; thank goodness He has given us the precious gift of Jesus, the Suffering Servant, the One we truly need.

Reflect

1. What sticks out to you the most in this description of the Savior?

2. Why might that have been surprising to the people?

3. Why do we need Jesus?

Pray

Lord, the greatest gift You could ever give is Jesus. Help us to accept the gift of Your grace, in Him, that we might be saved from our sin.

A King's Folly

Show

Place a bowl about six feet away from where you ask the family to stand. Give each one a piece of cereal, and ask them to see if they can pitch the cereal into the bowl. Separate the ones who make it on the first try, then have them all take a step backward and repeat until there is only one winner. The winner, at this point, will have successfully gotten the cereal into the bowl multiple times. Ask them if they are confident if they pitched the cereal again, they would make it again. Then ask them if they are confident they could make ten cereal pieces in a row. Explain that life works this way sometimes. Sometimes, something good happens, and we just assume that it will keep happening. This is a dangerous thing for us because when we do this in real life, it can mean we aren't trusting God for the future; we are trusting in ourselves and our own abilities. Transition to the next portion of the story, telling the family that this is what happened to King Hezekiah.

Read

2 Kings 20:12–21

Explain

King Hezekiah had a pattern of trusting in the Lord. In fact, God had just finished blessing Hezekiah not only by healing him from a life-threatening illness, but by giving him a miraculous sign that He would do so. But Hezekiah, instead of continuing to rely on and trust in the Lord, began to rely on himself. He became prideful—so prideful, in fact, that when a group came from Babylon, the king boastfully showed them everything he had. Isaiah came again to Hezekiah and gave him the Word of the Lord, that because of his pride, all those things the king was so proud of would eventually be carried off to Babylon. Isaiah was telling the king that eventually Judah would fall just like Israel, at the hands of the Babylonians. Though this would not happen in Hezekiah's lifetime, it would indeed happen just as God promised.

How tragic that the king, who had received so much from the Lord, chose to trust in himself instead of God. And how tragic it would be if we, who have received so much from the Lord, start trusting in anything else except the God who provides for us. We must remain vigilant in our faith, humbly recognizing that it is God alone who can provide for us and sustain us into the future.

Reflect

1. What did Hezekiah do when the group from Babylon came to visit him?

2. Why was that wrong?

3. Why is pride so dangerous in our own lives?

Pray

Lord, please guard us from pride so we will always humbly remember that You are the One who gives us everything we need.

The King Who Remembered

Show

Prior to family devotion, search through your attic or storage space and try to find a toy that your children once played with, but not in a long time. Bring the toy with you to family devotion time and ask for people to share specific memories of that toy. After they have a chance to do so, ask them why they don't play with it any more. Point out that this is the natural way of things—we enjoy something for a time, but eventually we move on. But there are some things that should never be forgotten; some things we should never just put in the closet. But that's what happened as the story continues. The people of Judah, and their kings, put away the law of God. Until one day, they found it again.

Read

2 Kings 22:3–12

Explain

The faithful days of King Hezekiah were long in the past. King after king came and went over the nation of Judah, and with each one the people drifted further and further from God. They drifted so much, in fact, that no one even read the law of the Lord any more. But then a new king rose to power. Josiah became king over Judah when he was only eight years old, and as he grew, he wanted to live faithfully to the God of his ancestors. After he had been king for eighteen years, some work was being done on the long-neglected temple, and the workers stumbled upon an old copy of the law of God. Josiah ordered it to be read, and it quickly became apparent just how sinful the people had become.

This is what happens when we read God's law—it functions like a mirror, showing us our actions, but also revealing our hearts. The law of God makes us fall on the mercy of God, asking Him for His grace, and that's what happened in Judah. The people returned to the Lord. Idols were destroyed, and for a time, the people lived faithfully. But despite this period of faithfulness, they would soon return to their idolatrous ways. The people didn't just need a change in action; they needed a change of heart that only God can provide.

Reflect

1. How was Josiah different than the kings who came before him?

2. What happened when they found and read God's law?

3. What effect should reading God's law have on us today?

Pray

Thank You, Lord, for the gift of the Bible. Help us to read it honestly, with open hearts, and receive what You show us in its pages.

Set Apart

Show

Bring some baby pictures of your family with you to family devotion. Allow the family to flip through the pictures, commenting on what you remember about each one. Then comment on how the children have grown and changed since these pictures—how you did not know everything they would face and become when those pictures were taken. But then explain that even though you didn't know, God did. In fact, God not only knew but planned the way they would grow up. Explain that you will see the same thing in the next part of the story.

Read

Jeremiah 1:4–10

Explain

During the days of King Josiah, God raised up a new prophet to speak His word. The prophet's name was Jeremiah. Jeremiah would prophesy long after the reign of King Josiah, and would bear witness to the eventual destruction of Judah. All these things God planned even before Jeremiah was born. In fact, God set Jeremiah apart for this prophetic ministry even before His birth.

Like Jeremiah, each one of us is born with a purpose. We all have a part to play in God's story, and God knows and plans that part even before our birth. That means each one of us is important, unique, and worthy of respect and honor. It also means that no role is insignificant to God. Whether you are someone in the spotlight like Jeremiah or someone in the shadows, you matter to God and His purposes. It's only when we understand our place in God's story and surrender to it that we really find who we are.

Reflect

1. Who was Jeremiah?

2. What did God say about Jeremiah's mission and message?

3. What does that mean about each one of us today?

Pray

God, You made us all on purpose, and with a purpose. Help us to know our place in Your story and surrender to the life You have planned for us.

The New Covenant

Show

Before family devotion, go outside and find a rock. With a marker, write the word *covenant* on the rock and bring it with you to family devotion. Pass the rock around, asking the family to feel it and make comments about its appearance. Point out the obvious with them—a rock is hard by its nature. While you might write a word on it, the word doesn't change the structure of the rock—it only exists on the surface. Transition to the next portion of the story by explaining that up until now, God's covenant with His people was written on stone, as in the Ten Commandments. But through Jeremiah, God was making a promise to do something brand-new.

Read

Jeremiah 31:31–34

Explain

A covenant is a special promise God makes, one that He binds Himself to keep. He made a covenant with Noah, a covenant with Abraham, and a covenant with David. But as He spoke through His prophet, Jeremiah, He promised to make a new kind of covenant. God had made a covenant with the nation of Israel on Mount Sinai, writing that covenant on stone. This was the law of God. But that law was something for the people to keep, not something that changed the people. And, of course, they were not able to live up to their part of that agreement. But God had a plan to do something new.

His new covenant would not be written on stone, as a set of laws for people to obey, but instead would be written on their hearts. God promised that in this new covenant, He would not just give a set of laws, but actually change His people from the inside out. He would make us brand-new, with new hearts—hearts that weren't committed to sin, but instead committed to following Him.

This is the only way we can truly be rescued from our sin—it's not by obeying the law, but instead by having a new, clean heart that loves God. This new heart only comes by God's grace, through our faith in Jesus Christ. When we trust in Jesus, the Holy Spirit of God gives us this new heart, and as we will see, the change is so big that it's like being born all over again.

Reflect

1. How did God write the old covenant?

2. What is different about the new covenant?

3. How can we receive a new heart?

Pray

God, thank You for being willing to change us from the inside out. Help us to understand and embrace this gift of a new heart that You are offering us through Jesus.

A City in Ruins

Show

As everyone gathers together, ask them to imagine that the family has decided to move. But the problem is, you only have one minute to be out of the house before you leave forever, and there's only time to grab one thing. Set a timer for one minute, then deploy the family to grab their one thing and be back together before the timer goes off. Allow each person to share what they grabbed, and why they chose that thing. Of course, they will be glad this wasn't real, but then transition to the next part of the story. Explain that you are about to enter into a difficult part of the story in which God's people would experience His judgment. They would be forced to leave their homeland, which God had promised them, not knowing if they would ever return.

Read

2 Kings 25:1–9

Explain

The northern kingdom of Israel had already been destroyed, but the southern kingdom of Judah would not escape God's judgment either. Despite a couple of good, faithful kings like Hezekiah and Josiah, Judah had continued in her idolatry. As a result, God did what He promised He would do—He brought judgment on the land using the Babylonian army, and the judgment was terrible. After months of being surrounded by the Babylonian army, and having nothing go in or out of the city, Jerusalem finally fell and was left in ruins. God's temple was destroyed along with everything else. Some of the survivors were taken captive and deported to a different land.

Surely the people had all kinds of questions. They must have wondered if God had left them. Or if they had any hope for the future. Or if the promises God had made Abraham and those who came after them were still good. While we see in this part of the story that God will not share His worship with anyone or anything else, we will also see that God had not abandoned His people. He would still make good on everything He promised them, including rescuing them not only from the Babylonians, but also from their sin.

Reflect

1. What happened to Jerusalem?

2. Why did it happen?

3. What can we learn from this part of the story?

Pray

Lord, help us to see just how serious You are about Your worship. Help us to take this seriously, knowing that You will judge those who do not choose to follow You alone.

 **Day 3**

A Lament for God's People

Show

Ask the family, one at a time, to name a song that when they hear it, it makes them feel better. After each person has a chance to share, explain that music is powerful in this way. God made us in such a way that our hearts connect with music. Songs can make us feel happy or sad, depending on what the song makes us remember. And while the next part of the story we will read is not a song, it can have the same effect.

Read

Lamentations 3:19–26

Explain

The book of Lamentations is a collection of poems written by the prophet Jeremiah. Jeremiah saw what happened to Judah and the city of Jerusalem, and one of the ways he expressed his sadness was through these poems. Jeremiah is actually nicknamed "the weeping prophet" because of how sad these times were for God's people. But even in the midst of his sadness, Jeremiah knew he could count on God. Despite what had happened, God had not abandoned His people. He would remain faithful to them, even though they had not been faithful to Him.

Week 29

This is good news for us today because we will all fall short of God's plan for our lives. We all sin. But God's mercy is greater than our sin. He will remain faithful to us even when we are not faithful to Him.

Reflect

1. What sticks out to you the most from this part of Lamentations?

2. How do you see both Jeremiah's sadness and his hope in these verses?

3. Why is this part of Lamentations still hopeful to us, even though it is sad?

Pray

Thank You, Lord, that Your mercies are new every morning. Help us to remember that Your grace and mercy are greater than our sin.

A Foreign Land

Show

Decide, as a family, what one sports team your family is the biggest fan of. To demonstrate this, you might gather posters, hats, T-shirts, or anything else in the house that represents this team and display them before the family. Then ask the family how they would feel if one day they were forced not only to stop wearing these things and cheering for your team, but instead to cheer for the arch rival. Obviously it would take some getting used to. Transition to the next portion of the story by reminding the family that Judah had been destroyed, but not all the people in the city had died. In fact, some of them were taken to Babylon, and they were being forced to adjust to a different way of life.

Read

Daniel 1:1–7

Explain

Jerusalem was destroyed, and Nebuchadnezzar, the king of Babylon, had taken the best and the brightest citizens of Judah as captives. Like their ancestor Joseph who was taken to Egypt, these people found themselves living in a foreign land and had to learn to live there. They were expected to fully adopt all the customs of Babylon, from language to food to manners.

At this point in the story we meet Daniel and his three friends that we know as Shadrach, Meshach, and Abednego. Though they were Hebrews, they had been taken into the service of the king of Babylon. Some difficult choices lay ahead of these three as they would have to choose to live as citizens of Babylon, or live as the people of the God of Israel.

In a way, we are in a similar situation. The Bible will later tell us that this world is not our home; rather, we are already citizens of heaven though we are living here. And we, too, must choose how to live—either the same as the citizens of the world, or as citizens of God's kingdom.

Reflect

1. Who were Daniel and his three friends?

2. What choices were they going to have to make?

3. How are we like Daniel and his friends?

Pray

Thank You, Lord, that You have made us citizens of another world. Help us to live as citizens of Your kingdom even though we are alive on earth.

Faithful in Food

Show

Gather together a few packages of food in the house. Make sure each package or can has an ingredient list. Distribute the items to different members of the family, and ask each one to read some of the ingredients on the list. They might be surprised at the variety of ingredients, many of which they might not have heard of. Explain that often we don't think about what the food we eat is actually made of. But in the next part of the story, we will see that Daniel was very concerned about the food he was being given to eat. But it wasn't just because he wanted to be healthy; it was because he wanted to be faithful.

Read

Daniel 1:8–16

Explain

Daniel was among those who had been taken into Babylon, but once there, he found himself in an interesting position. Rather than be treated as a slave or prisoner, he and his friends were brought into the palace and given the food and drink of the king. The intent was that the Hebrews would learn the ways of Babylon and become a part of the nation. But Daniel was so focused on being faithful to God that it even drove his decisions about what to eat. God had given His people rules and regulations about what was clean and unclean, and Daniel was not willing to violate God's law even though he was in a strange land. Daniel was willing to put his choice to the test, and the test showed not only that Daniel was faithful, but he was actually healthier as a result.

God gives us commands because He loves us. He has purpose in His direction, and when we are faithful to Him, we find that it is for our own good. But we should not only obey God because we think it will end well; we should obey God because He is God. Sometimes we immediately experience the good that comes from obeying God, but sometimes it doesn't look like it's going to turn out so great. In fact, the earthly consequences for obeying God can be severe, as the Hebrews would soon discover.

Reflect

1. What choice did Daniel make about the food of Babylon?

2. Why did he make that choice?

3. What does this show us about God's commands and why we should obey them?

Pray

Lord, thank You that You give commands out of love. Help us to obey You because we trust You and know that You love us.

A Choice to Stand

Show

As the family gathers together, present a coin before them. Explain that you will have a contest to see which member of the family can call either heads or tails correctly the most times out of ten coin flips. Flip the coin ten times with each family member calling heads or tails each time, keeping a record of who was correct. Then point to the fact that this was a simple choice—head or tails. Either choice was fine; it really didn't mean much. Sometimes choices in life are like this—we have two options, and we just need to choose one or the other. But sometimes choices are much more serious. These are choices between good and evil, right and wrong, faith or disbelief. In the next part of the story, we will see that Shadrach, Meshach, and Abednego were presented with one such choice.

Read

Daniel 3:8–18

Explain

God had shown favor to Daniel and the three friends, Shadrach, Meshach, and Abednego. Though they were from Judah, they had been appointed to positions of strength and power in Babylon, and not everyone was happy about it.

Nebuchadnezzar, king of Babylon, made a huge golden idol and required everyone to bow down and worship it. But when the three Hebrews refused, some of the government officials who were jealous of them reported it to the king knowing that the consequence of their actions was to be death. Shadrach, Meshach, and Abednego had to make a choice, and it was a choice with consequences. Even though they knew the punishment for their actions was death, they also knew they had to obey God and not men. As they stood before the king, they knew God could miraculously save them, but even if He did not, they still would not choose to worship something else.

This is what faith really looks like—making a choice and trusting God with the results. Even today, we are confronted with choices. We must decide in both big and small ways whether we will worship and obey God or not. Many of those choices come with consequences, but even after we make our choice, we must continue to trust in God for what happens next.

Centuries later, Jesus would have to make a choice. He would have to choose whether He would obey His Father and go to the cross, or whether He would go His own way. Thankfully, Jesus chose the way of courage and faith, trusting God with the results.

Reflect

1. What choice was presented to Shadrach, Meshach, and Abednego?

2. How did they show faith in their response to the king?

3. What is a difficult choice you have had to make recently?

Pray

We will all make choices today, Lord. Help us to make choices of faithfulness and trust You with what happens next.

The Fourth in the Fire

Show

To start the devotion, you will need a book of matches, a small piece of paper, and a bowl. Very carefully, light the piece of paper on fire with a match and let it fall into the bowl. Once it's mostly burned up, ask the family what some of the effects of the fire was. They will likely point out the texture of the paper, the way the color changed, and the smell. Affirm these observations, explaining that this is what happens when fire is involved. Then transition to the next part of the story by explaining that in order for these things to not happen, something miraculous would have to take place.

Read

Daniel 3:19–30

Explain

Shadrach, Meshach, and Abednego stood their ground. Confident in God alone, they refused to bow to the idol, so the king did as he promised. The three friends were thrown into a furnace so hot that the fire killed the guards that tossed them in.

But God was with Shadrach, Meshach, and Abednego, and as the king stood watching the scene, he observed not three but four people in the midst of the fire. Likewise, when we find ourselves in the midst of difficulty, we can know that God has not left us; He is actually with us even during times of sadness and pain. Shadrach, Meshach, and Abednego emerged from the fire with no effect. They were not burned at all, and they didn't even smell like smoke. As a result of their faithfulness, the entire kingdom heard about the greatness of their God. This is the end result of our faithfulness as well, and it should be our goal—that all people, everywhere, come to know and worship God alone.

Reflect

1. How were Shadrach, Meshach, and Abednego saved from the fire?

2. What was the result of their faithfulness?

3. How does this part of the story help us trust God?

Pray

You alone are God. You are more powerful than any fire, or anything else we face in life. Thank You that You will be with us no matter what we go through.

The Lions' Den

Show

Explain that the next part of the story is one of the best-known Bible stories in the world—the story of Daniel being thrown into the lions' den. To introduce this part of the story, share these three interesting facts with the family about lions:

- The average male lion weighs around 400 pounds while the average female lion weighs around 290 pounds.
- The roar of a lion can be heard from 5 miles away.
- A lion can run for short distances at 50 mph and leap as far as 36 feet.

Explain that facts like these help us appreciate just how dangerous the situation was for Daniel. But it's also important for us to remember how and why Daniel was thrown into the lions' den.

Read

Daniel 6:10–18

Explain

Years had passed since Daniel and the other Hebrews had been brought to Babylon. Babylon had now been conquered by Persia, and a new king, Darius, once again saw how wise and valuable Daniel was. But as happened with Shadrach, Meshach, and Abednego, there were other advisors who were jealous of Daniel's position. They knew the only way Daniel could be discredited was if there was a law that contradicted his faithfulness to God. That way, he would either have to abandon his faithfulness to God, or—more likely—break the law. So they persuaded Darius the king to pass a law requiring all the land to pray to the king alone. Instead of obeying this law, Daniel continued to regularly pray to God, and even though it saddened the king, he was bound by his own decree to throw Daniel into a pit of lions.

Like his three friends, Daniel made a choice and trusted the results to God. And like his three friends, God delivered Daniel. Once again we see that God is faithful. We can trust him with the results when we stand in faithfulness for what is right. God closed the mouths of the lions and delivered His servant Daniel, and through Christ, He delivers us from a much greater danger—the danger of sin.

Reflect

1. How did Daniel show his faith in God?

2. What were the consequences of Daniel's actions?

3. What is one way we will have to choose to stand for God today?

Pray

You are the Lord over all creation. You deliver from the fire, and You close the mouths of lions. Help us to trust You when it is costly to stand in faithfulness.

Faith in Action

Show

As the family gathers together, place a chair in front of them and ask for a volunteer. Ask the volunteer if he or she believes that sitting in the chair is safe. When they answer "yes," ask them how the rest of the family can know they are telling the truth. In other words, how can the rest of the family know the volunteer really believes the chair is safe? The obvious answer is for the volunteer to sit in the chair. Explain that the action of sitting in the chair proves the words of faith. Further explain that the Bible teaches us that faith and actions are always linked together. If we believe something, then our actions will show it. Explain that this is one of the things we see as the story continues.

Read

Nehemiah 2:1–7

Explain

Faith is the most important part of our lives. Faith should be the center of everything we do. But how do we know if that faith is real? By our actions.

This is what we see from Nehemiah. Nehemiah knew the walls of Jerusalem were still in ruins from when the Babylonians attacked the city. This was important because the walls were the means of safety and protection for the city. Nehemiah was sad, but in his sadness, he took action. He spent time praying about the problem he saw, and his faith then motivated him to further action. When he had the opportunity, he spoke to the king, and God gave him favor. The king amazingly agreed to everything Nehemiah asked for, and he went to undertake the project of rebuilding the walls.

Like Nehemiah, we will look and see big problems all over the world. We will see hurting and suffering people all around us. We should have faith in God, and that faith should motivate us to action. We must be ready not just to believe, but to show our faith by putting action to it when we have the opportunity.

Reflect

1. What was the problem that concerned Nehemiah?

2. What did Nehemiah believe, and what did he do?

3. What are some examples of actions we can take today that show our faith is real?

Pray

Lord, help us to be people of faith. And help us to remember that our actions will show whether our faith is real.

The Miraculous Wall

Show

Explain to the family that the kids will have an arm-wrestling contest. Pair them up, and allow them to arm-wrestle each other until you have one winner. Then talk about the contest, helping the family to see that when you are wrestling like this, one person is trying to push the other person's arm down while the other person is trying desperately to keep it from happening. It is an illustration of a person trying to keep another person from achieving their goals. Explain that this is what happened when Nehemiah went to rebuild the wall. He faced great opposition in the task.

Read

Nehemiah 6:15–16

Explain

Nehemiah had everything he needed in the way of supplies, and he was able to rally the people in Jerusalem to actually do the work. But the task would not come easy. At every turn, Nehemiah faced opposition from other leaders in the area who wanted to make sure that Jerusalem did not become a powerful and safe city again. But Nehemiah persevered, and he led the people to persevere. People stood guard while the work took place, sometimes building with one hand and holding a sword in the other. In the end, the walls were rebuilt in miraculous fashion—a job that should have taken much, much longer. It only happened because God was with His people, empowering them to do the task.

When we face a task that seems too big, we might think about walking away. But we would do well to remember that perseverance is one of the markers of Christians. We are the people who keep going when we know what we are doing is right. All the while, we must trust in God who will give us the strength we need to do what is right, and even when we fail in the task we hope to accomplish, we can know that God will use it to make us more like His Son.

Reflect

1. Why was building the wall such a difficult task?

2. How long did it take the people to get the job done?

3. What does this part of the story teach us about perseverance?

Pray

Thank You, Lord, that You give strength to Your people. Help us to continue to trust in You when the task before us is difficult.

An Orphan to a Queen

Show

As the family gathers together, ask each person to share their favorite "rags to riches" story. Some examples might be Annie or Cinderella. After each person shares, transition to the next part of the story. Explain that God's people were still in a foreign land, making their way as best they could. This is when we meet a young orphan named Esther who would eventually become a queen.

Read

Esther 2:1–10

Explain

By this time, the Hebrews were now part of the Persian kingdom, as the Persians had defeated the Babylonians. The evil king had become upset with the queen and set about looking for a new queen to take her place. All the young women were gathered together as candidates for the new queen, and among them was an orphan named Esther. She was very beautiful, and she was chosen to be presented before the king. But Esther had a secret. Her uncle Mordecai, who raised her, had told her not to tell anyone that she was a Hebrew. Perhaps Mordecai thought that she would be mistreated if people knew where she came from and who her ancestors were. So even as she was becoming the new queen, she kept this secret from everyone. While it might seem like on the surface that Esther was just lucky, God was actually at work. He was moving Esther into a position of power so that He could use her to save her people from destruction.

God is always at work in our lives and in the world. We can know, by faith, that in any situation we find ourselves, God has chosen for us to be there so that we, too, might play a role in His story.

Reflect

1. Who were Esther and Mordecai?

2. What was Esther's secret?

3. How was God working behind the scenes?

Pray

Help us to have faith, Lord, in Your plan and work. Help us to know that You are moving us into positions and situations to play our part in Your story.

A Villain Emerges

Show

As the family gathers together, remind them of how in the last devotion they shared their favorite "rags to riches" stories. Ask them today to share their best villain. It might be a villain from a movie, a book, or a comic book. After each person shares, ask them to think about the question a little more, asking them what makes a good villain. Then transition to today's part the story, explaining that you saw how God was moving Esther into a position of importance. At the same time, though, a villain was emerging in the story—one that would threaten the lives and future of God's people.

Read

Esther 3:1–6

Explain

Mordecai would not bow down. We don't know exactly why; perhaps he knew something of Haman's character. But whatever the reason, Mordecai stood his ground rather than honor Haman, and Haman was enraged. He didn't just want to punish Mordecai; he wanted to seek revenge on all Mordecai's people. Haman set about hatching a plan by which all of God's people would be killed, and he put his plan into action.

As evil as Haman was, he is just a reflection of a greater villain. We first met the greater villain in the garden, and this villain is full of pride, vengeance, and evil too. Like Haman, the devil is seeking to do harm to all God's people. To defeat this villain, the Hebrews needed a hero to emerge, and so do we. We need someone to step in, take action, and ensure the defeat of the villain. And in both cases, God provided such a hero.

Reflect

1. Why was Haman so angry at Mordecai?

2. What did he plan to do?

3. How does Haman point us to the greater villain in the story?

Pray

You tell us, Lord, that we have an enemy that prowls like a lion looking for someone to devour. Thank You that Jesus is the hero we need, the One who can bring destruction upon the enemy.

Taking Action

Show

Explain to the family that you are going to play a game of "Trust Fall." Ask for a volunteer. The volunteer will stand, back straight, with their arms crossed and eyes closed. You will stand behind them, and they will fall backward, without moving their arms or bending their back, and you will catch them. Repeat the exercise a couple of times, and the family will probably be surprised at how difficult it is to keep their back straight and not try to stop themselves from falling. But then transition to the next part of the story by explaining that if you really trust someone, then you will be willing to take a risk knowing that person will help you. When you last left the story of Esther, Haman had put into motion a terrible plan to kill all the Israelites. Esther, who was by that time the queen, would have to make a choice. But her choice would come with great risk.

Read

Esther 4:10–17

Explain

Haman's evil plan was in motion, but despite the odds against them, Mordecai believed God would not forsake His people. He challenged Queen Esther to believe the same thing. He wanted

Esther to take action, but her action would require great risk. At that time, no one appeared before the king unless he asked them to, and if Esther went before the king, she very well might be killed. But Mordecai wanted Esther to see that God had intentionally put her in this position of power and influence, not only for her own good, but for the good of her people.

Esther would indeed take the chance, and eventually Haman's evil plot was exposed. Haman was put to death for his treachery, and the people of God were saved. All this happened because one woman was willing to believe in God and take a chance. For us today, taking action will also require risk. We must challenge ourselves, just as Mordecai challenged Esther, to see if we really believe God has intentionally put us in the school, neighborhood, and jobs we are in. We aren't in these places by accident, but instead "for such a time as this." But not only should we look to Esther, we should also remember Jesus, who had His own moment. He had to choose to believe that God was in control, and doing so would cost Him His life.

Reflect

1. Why was Esther's choice a risky one?

2. What did Mordecai have to believe to encourage Esther this way?

3. What is one chance you think God might be wanting you to take for Him?

Pray

Lord, You don't do anything by accident. Help us to believe that we are in our neighborhoods, schools, and relationships on purpose so we can influence people with the good news of Jesus.

The Dry Bones

Show

Prior to family devotion, gather together a random bunch of Legos, building blocks, or other construction toys. Put them before the family, and give them three minutes to use the blocks to create something. After time expires, allow the family to point out different aspects of the structure, then ask them what else they might have made if they had more time. Encourage their responses, then explain that they could have built all kinds of things using the blocks. But the blocks could not build themselves. They are just blocks, incapable of creativity, movement, and life. Then transition to the next part of the story by introducing Ezekiel, a prophet who lived when God's people were removed from their homeland. Explain that God showed Ezekiel a vision of dry bones which, much like these blocks, could not move themselves—but then, something miraculous happened.

Read

Ezekiel 37:1–10

Explain

It was an amazing—and strange—vision. The valley full of bones was laid out before Ezekiel, and God asked His prophet an obvious question: "Can these dry bones live?" Of course, the answer was no, but Ezekiel knew all things are possible with God, so he responded to the question with the correct answer: "You alone know." That's because God can do anything, and only He knows what He is going to do. Before Ezekiel's eyes, the valley of bones started to move and eventually came to life.

The vision is meant to represent what God would do not only with His people of Israel, but all those who believe in Jesus. The Bible tells us that we are all dead in our sin. Like the valley of bones, we can't change our situation, but God can. When we believe in Jesus, God gives us new spiritual life—we are born again. Just as it happened to the valley of bones, it can happen in each of our hearts if we believe in Jesus.

Reflect

1. What did Ezekiel see in his vision?

2. What was God's question, and how did Ezekiel respond?

3. How are we like the valley of bones?

Pray

Thank You, Lord, that You can make the dead live again. Help us to believe in Jesus so that we might have new life.

 **Day 3**

Bought Back

Show

Bring several wedding pictures, if you are married, with you to family devotion. If not, try and fine some wedding pictures from another couple in your family. As you are able, tell some stories to the family about the pictures. Include what you were wearing, what you were thinking, and other details about the wedding celebration. Then ask the family to share their own reflections on some of the things people might feel at their wedding. Generally, weddings are very happy occasions, but there was a wedding in the Bible that was different. Remind the family that God's people were still away from their homeland because they were unfaithful to Him. It was during this time that God called another prophet, Hosea, to do something very strange.

Read

Hosea 3:1–3

Explain

Most of the time God gave His prophets words to speak. They delivered God's message with words. But sometimes, God worked differently, and in the case of Hosea, the prophet's whole life would be the message. God told Hosea to marry a woman who would not be faithful to him. Time after time, she would

268

leave her husband for other men, and time after time Hosea would take her back.

God wanted Hosea's life to be a picture of what it was like for Him, for His people had time after time worshiped other gods. Eventually, Hosea's wife, Gomer, actually became a slave and Hosea had to go and buy her back. The word for this buying back is *redemption*. God was showing His people that there was a price for their sin, just as there is a price for ours. The price for our sin is death—that is what we deserve for our disobedience. But just as Hosea paid the price to redeem his unfaithful wife, God was also willing to pay the price to buy us back from our sin. The price, in this case, was not a bag of silver, but the death of His Son, Jesus. Because God loves us, He redeems us with His Son.

Reflect

1. How was Hosea's ministry different than some of the other prophets?

2. What did Hosea have to do for Gomer?

3. What does this show us about what God is willing to do for us?

Pray

We know, Lord, there is a high price for our sin. Thank You for being willing to buy us back with the death of Jesus.

The Spirit to Come

Show

As the family gathers together, lay out before them a credit card, debit card, or both. Ask the family if they know what the cards are, and what they are used for. Briefly explain what they are if the kids don't know, and then ask them who carries the cards. Explain that you would not give the card to one of the children to carry with them all the time, because handling the finances of the family is primarily for the adults. There are certain things like that—responsibilities that are just for the adults. Remind the family that up to this point in the story, the Spirit of God had been given to a select few people. But that was going to change.

Read

Joel 2:28–29

Explain

We have seen the Holy Spirit before. He was there, hovering over the earth at creation. And we saw the Spirit give Samson incredible strength. It was the Spirit who transported Ezekiel to the valley. But Joel, the prophet, told of a day when the Spirit would not just be for a few, but for all. Previously, the Spirit of God was given to a single person for a single purpose, and then the Spirit would leave. But according to Joel, a day was coming when the Spirit would be given to the young and the old, the rich and the poor.

Joel was talking about something that happens when someone becomes a Christian. When someone becomes a Christian, the Holy Spirit of God lives inside of them. The Spirit is an incredible gift God gives, but He is a gift only for those who believe in Jesus. It's an incredible mystery, but God has and will always exist in three persons—the Father, the Son, and the Holy Spirit. All three are one God, and yet all three do different things. It's through His Spirit that God not only gives us power and strength, but also fulfills His desire to live as closely as possible with the people He loves.

Reflect

1. So far, how have we seen the Holy Spirit work?

2. How was what Joel described different?

3. How do we experience the Holy Spirit today?

Pray

Thank You, God, for the incredible gift of the Holy Spirit. Help us to recognize the Spirit within us and walk as He directs us.

The Prophet Who Ran

Show

As the family gathers together, challenge them to have a conversation using nothing but opposite terms. For example, you might greet them by saying, "Bad morning," and telling them, "I hope you're doing badly this morning." Ask the family how hard it was to say the opposite of what they were thinking. Then transition to the next part of the story by explaining that today you will meet a prophet who didn't just say the opposite of what he was thinking; he actually did the opposite of what God told him to do.

Read

Jonah 1:1–17

Explain

Jonah heard the call of God, but it was not a call he wanted or expected. Though he was a prophet and had heard the Word of the Lord before, in this case, Jonah did not obey. God called him to go to the city of Nineveh. He was to preach to the enemies of the Hebrews, the people who had been cruel and violent toward them. Jonah knew that if the people repented, God would spare them, and since he hated the Ninevites, he did not want that to happen. Rather than obeying God's call, Jonah went in the exact opposite direction on a boat.

But God would not allow His prophet to live in that kind of disobedience. With all nature at His command, God raised up a storm and Jonah was tossed overboard. Even still, God would not let the prophet go his own way, and so He caused a fish to swallow him whole, which would preserve Jonah's life long enough for what would come next.

God has told us how we should live, and that we should work to share the good news of His kingdom. When we choose to live in disobedience to God, God will discipline us just as He did Jonah. That's one of the ways we know that God loves us—He loves us too much to allow us to go our own way.

Reflect

1. Why did Jonah disobey God's call?

2. How did God discipline Jonah?

3. Why is God's discipline evidence of His love for us?

Pray

Thank You, Lord, that You love us too much to allow us to live in disobedience. When we know You are disciplining us, help us to be quick to repent and return to You.

The Prophet Preaches

Show

As the family gathers together, go around the circle and ask each person to share their least favorite subject in school, and why. Affirm that every subject can't be our favorite, and inevitably we have to go through a class we don't enjoy. But even when we don't enjoy that class, we still show up, study, and try to power through it. When we last left Jonah, he had been swallowed by a fish, but we will see that Jonah would eventually do his job of preaching. But even as he did, he was just completing the task. His heart wasn't in what he was doing.

Read

Jonah 2:8–3:10

Explain

By any measure, Jonah's preaching was an incredible success. After receiving the discipline from the Lord, Jonah was spit up right where God wanted him to be, and after God gave him the instructions a second time, Jonah went and preached a simple message to the people. The people heard the word of the Lord and responded with repentance. The king ordered a national period of sorrow and mourning; the people humbled themselves before God, and God saw their repentance. Because God is rich in mercy, He did not execute judgment on the Ninevites.

Thankfully, God is merciful to us as well. When we hear God's Word and repent, He always has grace for us. But that leaves the question of God's prophet. He had done what God told him to do, at least in action. But as we will see, Jonah's heart was far from excited about what happened.

We might fall into the same pattern of doing the right things, but with hearts that are still far from God. We don't just need to be obedient to God's Word; we need new hearts that delight in obedience. We can only have that new heart through Jesus.

Reflect

1. What was Jonah's message to the people?

2. What happened?

3. Why is it important for us not just to obey God, but to want to obey God?

Pray

Lord, we don't just want to obey; we want to love You. Thank You for the gift of a new heart we can have through Jesus Christ.

The Angry Prophet

Show

Prior to gathering for family devotion, go outside and pick a few weeds. Bring the weeds inside and display them before the family. Ask the family how they would respond if you took these weeds and made a place for them at the table. You would serve them a plate of food, and then at night take them to a bed in the house and tuck them in. Of course, the suggestion is silly because you would never do for the weeds what you would do for a family member. Transition to the next part of the story by explaining that as silly as this is, it is not far from what we see happening next in the story of Jonah.

Read

Jonah 4:1–11

Explain

Jonah knew what would happen. He knew the character of God, that He is slow to anger and abounding in love, and He knew that if the people repented, God would show them grace. The idea made the prophet angry because, in his mind, the people of Nineveh were so wicked that they didn't deserve mercy. He did not want God to show them grace. As the story of Jonah closes, we see Jonah actually being more upset over a dying plant than over the thousands of people in Nineveh that God had spared!

Like Jonah, we might tend to look at people who are unkind to us, don't share our views, or are different than we are and think they don't deserve a chance to hear about God's grace. What we fail to realize in this is that none of us are worthy of God's grace. Jonah was just as sinful as the people he wanted to die. We are all in the same need of God's rescue. We should be careful, then, that we do not withhold the love and message of God's rescue from anyone around us just because we don't like them very much. The story of Jonah ends in a strange way; we don't know what happened to the prophet after this. Perhaps that's because Jonah's story is our story. Like him, we must choose whether we will join God in His story and mission to rescue all kinds of people, or whether we will not.

Reflect

1. Why was Jonah angry?

2. What did God use the plant to teach Jonah?

3. What are some of the lessons we learn from this part of the story?

Pray

Thank You, Lord, that You are abounding in mercy. You have showed us mercy; help us to remember how loving You are toward us so that we might love other people.

The Last Word ... for Now

Show

As the family devotion begins, show the family a picture. It can be a picture of anyone or anything, just as long as there are a lot of details in the picture. Ask them to look closely at the picture for about ten seconds, then flip it over and ask the family to recall every detail they can remember. You might have to prompt them with some questions: What was the picture of? Who was in it? What were they wearing? What was in the background? After a time of sharing those details, flip the picture back over and point out a few things the family did not remember. Explain that remembering is a difficult thing sometimes, but it's also really important. It's important when it comes to the story we have been reading as well. Unfortunately, it seems like the people of God have short memories. Explain that in the next part of the story, God told His people one more time to make sure they remembered what was most important.

Read

Malachi 4:4–6

Explain

Malachi is the last book of the Old Testament, and it is a book of both love and warnings. Time and time again in the book, God reminded His people of His love for them, but He also pointed out all the ways they had failed to remember Him. They failed to remember to bring the best animals for sacrifices. The priests failed to remember how to serve properly before the Lord. The people failed to remember the law and covenant the Lord had put before them. Judgment had come, and the people felt the pain of destruction, but God had not abandoned them. He promised that eventually, He would send them another prophet, like Elijah, who would give them another message and opportunity to repent and return to Him. But He also gave them a warning—there would eventually be a day when final judgment would come. And then it would be too late.

The people had a choice, as they always had—would they trust the Lord and turn to Him, or would they continue in their own way? Though it would be a long time, the people were going to receive God's final Word on the subject. And the Word that was coming was not written down or spoken; this time, the Word would be alive.

Reflect

1. What did God want the people to remember?

2. What would happen if they did not?

3. What do you think is going to happen next in the story?

Pray

Lord, help us to see Your warnings as evidence of Your love. Help us to take these warnings seriously and turn and trust in You.

In Between

Show

Gather the family together for family devotion, and announce that the devotion is going to begin. But then rather than saying anything, just sit in silence and look at the family for thirty seconds. You might be surprised at how difficult it is to sit in silence for that long. It can be uncomfortable, but make sure you don't speak. Then, after the thirty seconds is done, ask them how they felt during the silence. Transition to the next part of the story by reminding the family that the book of Malachi is the last book in the Old Testament. What happened next was 400 years of silence from God.

Read

We will not have a Bible passage during this devotion. Rather, we will consider some of the things that happened in between the end of the period of the Old Testament and the New Testament.

Explain

It was 400 years of silence. There were no prophets; there was no additional Word from God. And while the people might have wondered if God had abandoned them, His silence did not mean He was not busy. God was moving the pieces of history around, so that at just the right time Jesus would be born. Part of God's people had been allowed to return to their homeland, as we saw during the days of Nehemiah. Malachi also prophesied to these people who had returned. And during the 400 years, the number of people back in the land of Israel grew. But they were still not free. They had lived under the Babylonians, then the Persians, then the Greeks, and finally the Roman Empire. Even so, the people remembered that God had promised to send them a deliverer—a Messiah—and they were still looking for Him. Unfortunately, they were looking for someone who would bring freedom from the Babylonians. Or the Persians. Or the Greeks or the Romans. But God's Messiah would bring a much better kind of freedom than that.

Also during this time, a religious group called the Pharisees rose up among the people. They believed in strict adherence to the law, but also to laws they had added. When the New Testament opens, the Roman Empire had brought a stable government, slavery, and transportation to the land. For the first time, people could travel in safety across the known world. The stage was set; everything was ready. And as 400 years came to an end, the time had come for God to launch the next phase of His story. Jesus was going to be born.

Reflect

1. What do you think it was like for the people to not hear anything from God for 400 years?

2. How did some of these things make it the right time for Jesus to be born?

3. What are some of the ways you've seen in the story that God has been moving the whole story toward the birth of Jesus?

Pray

Lord, help us not mistake Your silence for Your absence. Thank You that in the Bible, we can now always hear a word from You. Help us to know that You are always at work.

The Silent Father

Show

Explain to the family that you will play a game together in which one member of the family tries to keep from laughing while the other family members try and get them to. The only rule is that no one can touch the person trying not to laugh. Play a few rounds of the game, then transition to the next part of the story by telling the family that though it might be difficult not to laugh, it was a choice on the part of the person not to do so. But in the next part of the story, you will read about a man who not only couldn't laugh, but couldn't speak. He couldn't speak not because he chose to be silent, but because he was kept from speaking by the power of God.

Read

Luke 1:5–20

Explain

After 400 years, the Lord's silence was broken. An angel appeared to a faithful priest named Zechariah who, along with his wife, had not been able to have children. Imagine the shock of this man when he not only saw an angel, but the angel told him he would have a son! And imagine his further shock when he learned that this child would be the child Malachi prophesied about, that he would have the Spirit of Elijah within him. Like Elijah hundreds of years earlier, this child, too, would issue warnings to the people of the need to repent and return to the Lord. Perhaps the news was just too much for Zechariah, because he couldn't believe what the messenger from heaven was saying. As a result, Zechariah would be prevented from speaking until his son was born, a sign that he had truly encountered the power of God. Though it had always been in His heart, God was now launching a new phase in His rescue plan. John would be born, and he would pave the way for the birth of Jesus.

Reflect

1. What would be special about Zechariah and Elizabeth's child?

2. Where do you see Zechariah's lack of belief?

3. How should we respond to God's Word when we read it?

Pray

Help us, Lord, to be people of faith that take You at Your Word. Help us to believe Your Word when we read and hear it.

A Willing Servant

Show

To begin today's family devotion, explain to the family that predictions are statements about the future. Ask each family member to make a prediction. The prediction might be about what you will have for dinner, who will win a sports game, or something else that will happen in the life of a family. After everyone has had a chance to make their predictions, remind the family that when we make predictions, all we are doing is guessing. Our guesses might be educated and reasonable, but there are still all kinds of things that can happen to destroy those predictions. Explain that prophecies in the Bible are much different than this. And in the next section of the story, you will read about how a prophesy from long ago was about to come true.

Read

Luke 1:26–38

Explain

Mary had no idea it was coming. She was an ordinary girl, and yet God had great plans for her. Though she was not married, she would become miraculously pregnant and give birth to a son. Like Zechariah, she received unbelievable news from an unbelievable source. She was going to be a pivotal part of a centuries-old prophecy, one that God intended to make good on.

Many years earlier, God had promised that a virgin would become pregnant and give birth to a son. The time had come for the prophecy to come true. But unlike Zechariah, Mary was willing to believe even what she didn't understand. Mary shows us the posture of a servant, someone who is ready to surrender their whole life, including their understanding, to the will of God.

Like her, we may read things in God's Word that we don't understand. We might hear promises of God that we don't see applying to us. But we have the opportunity to live by faith, not by sight, and trust that God will make good on His Word.

Reflect

1. How was Mary's response to the angel different than Zechariah's?

2. In your own words, what does it mean to have faith?

3. What are some obstacles to our faith right now?

Pray

Help us, Lord, to be willing servants. Help us to surrender all to You, including our need to understand everything.

The Real Hero

Show

Prior to family devotion, gather together a piece of paper and some markers, crayons, or colored pencils. Present the materials before the family, and explain that together you will create your own superhero, one characteristic at a time. Go first, and draw the outline of a person and include some superhero quality. For example, you might draw a cape to show the superhero can fly or big muscles to show how strong the superhero is. After you draw one characteristic, pass the paper to the next family member and allow them to add a characteristic by drawing it. Continue until every family member has had the chance to add their own characteristic. When finished, take a moment and reflect on the superhero you created. Then transition to the next part of the story by acknowledging that this would be a pretty great superhero, but the Bible gives us a picture not of a superhero, but of the hero we need. As we continue the story, that picture is becoming more and more clear.

Read

Matthew 1:18–25

Explain

Joseph didn't understand everything happening to him. He was engaged to Mary, but she had become pregnant even though they weren't yet married. Joseph was considering leaving Mary alone because he didn't understand how this could have happened. But he, too, got an unexpected visit from an angel who told him the truth of the situation. He was not to leave Mary, but instead should raise this child, for He was the hero the people needed. He would not just be Joseph's son, but God's Son, and He would save their people from their sins.

While we might imagine all kinds of heroes, we don't need a hero with superstrength, the power of flight, or X-ray vision. We need this hero because the danger we most need to be saved from is our sin.

Reflect

1. Why was Joseph confused?

2. What did the angel tell Joseph about the boy who would be born?

3. In what sense is Jesus a hero?

Pray

You have given us, Lord, the hero we need. Help us to trust in Jesus, for He alone can save us from our sin.

The Birth of Jesus

Show

To begin today's family devotion, share a few stories about when your children were born, focusing on all the preparations that had to be made for them. You might talk about things like baby showers, putting together cribs, and installing car seats. Emphasize the amount of work it took to get things ready for a new baby. Then transition to the next part of the story by reminding the family that having a baby requires a lot of preparation. In this case, God had been preparing the whole world since the garden of Eden. But even though God was prepared for the birth of His Son, Mary and Joseph were not. That's because they had to take a trip.

Read

Luke 2:1–7

Explain

Joseph was one of David's descendants, and the Roman ruler of the day required that everyone in the land return to the home of their family. That took Joseph and his pregnant wife back to David's hometown of Bethlehem. Remember how God had made a promise—a covenant—with David many years earlier? He promised that one of David's great-grandchildren would sit on the throne forever. Everything was coming together, and Jesus, the fulfillment of this covenant, was born in Bethlehem.

But this King was not born in a palace; his parents were not famous or powerful; in fact, there wasn't even a proper room for Him to be born in. The town was so crowded the only available place for the little family was a barn. But Jesus' birth shows us something about His mission. Just as He was born in an unexpected way for a king, so also would He have an unexpected mission for a king. Just as He was not born in a palace, neither would He sit on a throne in one. Jesus would sit on the throne of heaven, for He was not the earthly king many expected; He would be the heavenly King that everyone needed. And this King was not merely the son of Mary and Joseph, but He is God Himself, wrapped not just in blankets but in human flesh.

Reflect

1. Why were Mary and Joseph in Bethlehem?

2. How does Jesus' birth show us something about His mission?

3. How should we respond to the birth of Jesus?

Pray

What an amazing thing, Father, to think that Jesus came to earth and was born as a baby. Help us to feel a greater sense of joy knowing that the true King has come.

The First Visitors

Show

As the family gathers together, go around in a circle and allow each person to share what their dream job would be. Encourage each of the responses, and when you come to the end of the exercise, comment that usually when we are kids and think of dream jobs, we think of things that we would be good at, or things that would provide a large income, or things that would allow us to see different parts of the world. Now ask the family to imagine that you were all living in the days of the New Testament and were asked the same question. Probably very few people would answer the question with "shepherd," because a shepherd was not an important or well-respected job. But as you will see as the story continues, shepherds were the exact people who first heard the news of Jesus' birth.

Read

Luke 2:8–20

Explain

What a night it was. The shepherds no doubt remembered it the rest of their lives, for they not only heard the news about Jesus' birth, but they heard about it in dynamic and dramatic fashion. Unlike the single angel who visited both Mary and Joseph, this was a heavenly host, and it was indeed a message of great joy. On that night, God launched His rescue plan in earnest. The plan that had long been in His heart was unfolding, and it was starting with a tiny baby in a manger.

But why would God choose lowly shepherds, on this most important of nights and with this most important of messages, to be the first visitors to see His Son? Again, we see something here about the mission of Jesus. Throughout His life, Jesus would often befriend and walk with people that the rest of society didn't think were important. Though no one else did, Jesus always had time for people like this. There is no one unimportant to God; there is no one He is not willing to receive with grace and mercy. Even people like these shepherds.

Reflect

1. What sticks out to you the most about this part of the story?

2. What do you think the shepherds remembered most clearly from this night in the years that followed?

3. What do we learn about Jesus' mission from this part of the story?

Pray

Thank You, Lord, that there is no one unimportant to You. Help us to treat everyone with kindness and respect in light of that.

The Wise Men and the King

Show

Prior to family devotion today, do a quick internet search to find a celebrity, sports figure, or other well-known person whose birthday is today. Gather the names, and then as the family comes together, reveal the famous birthdays. Then comment on the fact that the family didn't buy gifts or throw parties for these people, and ask them why you didn't. Obviously, the family wouldn't throw a party for people they did not know. Parties and gifts are generally given to people who have personal contact with us. But then transition to the next part of the story, explaining that you will see today that Jesus is not just a Savior and Friend for a specific group of people, but for the whole world. That's why everyone should have the chance to celebrate Him.

Read

Matthew 2:1–12

Explain

We don't know how much time passed between the night Jesus was born and when the wise men presented their gifts to Him. It might have been just a few months, but it also might have been as long as two years. Whatever the case, these men took a long road to find the new King, though they, too, likely did not know exactly what kind of king He would be.

These were not Hebrews, but instead wise and educated men from foreign lands. Yet they assumed the same posture as the shepherds—one of honor and reverence. That's because Jesus is not just the King of the Jews; He's the King of kings. He came not just to save the people of God from the Old Testament, but to save people from all nations. This is God's rescue mission—it's not just for one group of people from one place, but for anyone who is willing to believe in Him and receive His grace and forgiveness.

Reflect

1. Why is it important to remember where the wise men came from?

2. How did they show honor and reverence for Jesus?

3. Why is it important for us to remember that Jesus is not just the Savior of one group of people, but the Savior of anyone who will have faith in Him?

Pray

Thank You, Lord, for the gift of Jesus. And thank You that He is powerful and willing to save any who come to Him.

On the Run

Show

As the family gathers together, share with them a story about when you have moved. It might be when you went to college, when you moved into your current house, or when you moved for another job. In your story, include details about why you moved, what was exciting, and what was difficult about the move. Allow the family to ask any questions about the story, and then explain that people move for all different kinds of reasons. But as the story continues, you will see that Mary, Joseph, and Jesus had to move not for something like a different job, but because of danger.

Read

Matthew 2:13–21

Explain

It was time for another heavenly message, but this time, it wasn't a message of joy but of warning. Yet again, a horrible tragedy was about to unfold in the land. Just as it was in the days of Moses, another ruler decreed that all the boys in the land less than two years old were to be killed. Herod had heard from the wise men about this king that was said to have been born, and he would not allow any challenge to his power. But

God would not allow His rescue plan to be ruined by a prideful king; He sent Mary and Joseph to Egypt for a time so that they and Jesus could be safe.

Throughout the story of history, many have thought they could derail God's plan. The good news of Jesus has been challenged with violence throughout the years, and yet God's plan and purpose have withstood. We can be confident, even today, that nothing and no one can stop God's plans. He will continue on, and we can be confident that God—and good—will win in the end.

Reflect

1. How was the angel's message different this time than the last?

2. Why did Mary and Joseph have to go to Egypt?

3. What does this show us about God and His plan?

Pray

Thank You, Lord, for protecting Your plan and purposes. Help us to remember that You will win in the end.

Wisdom and Stature

Show

On a piece of paper, write a series of simple addition problems and ask one of the children to work them. They should be easy enough to get through quickly. Then, below those problems draw out a much more complicated problem. For example:

$$f(x) = x^2 \ln x$$

Ask the child to work this problem, which should be obviously too difficult. Explain that someday, when he or she is older, she might take a calculus class and understand what this problem means and how to work it, but no one would expect him or her, at his or her age, to be able to solve that kind of problem. Transition to the next part of the story by explaining that Jesus was different. He was wise beyond His years, not in terms of math, but in terms of the way He understood God and the Scriptures.

Read

Luke 2:41–52

Explain

When it was safe, the family returned from Egypt and settled in Nazareth, but every year, the family would travel to Jerusalem. This was a common pattern during that time; Jewish people from all over the world would come to Jerusalem once a year to celebrate the Passover. But this year, when Jesus was twelve years old, was different. When the family left Jerusalem, they would have left in a large group. The group was so large that Mary and Joseph failed to notice that Jesus was not with them. When they returned to Jerusalem, they found Jesus in the temple, and He was showing the teachers of the law just how wise He was.

It was obvious to any who encountered Him that there was something special about this young man. It wasn't His physical appearance that marked Him, but rather His spirit. His heart. His understanding. Jesus knew, even then, that He had a different purpose than anyone else. God was His true Father, and He would spend His life in obedience to Him.

Reflect

1. Why was Jesus' family in Jerusalem?

2. Where was Jesus and what was He doing when Mary and Joseph found Him?

3. What does this show us about Jesus as a young man?

Pray

Thank You, God, that Jesus had no misunderstanding about His mission and purpose. Thank You for the obedient life and death of Jesus.

Repent!

Show

Explain to the family that you are going to play a few rounds of the game called "Rock, Paper, Scissors"—but with a slight twist. Two family members will start each round standing back to back, and on the count of three, they will jump and turn to face each other. When they do, they should either be making a piece of paper, with a flat hand, a rock, with a fist, or a pair of scissors with two fingers. The paper covers the rock, the rock smashes the scissors, and the scissors cut the paper. Play the game several times until only one family member remains who is the winner. Now focus on the part of the game that involves the turn. Turning was the key addition to this classic game, and in the next part of the story, you are going to hear a message that is just that simple: turn.

Read

Matthew 3:1–11

Explain

Like Jesus, John the Baptist knew his purpose. His mission in life was to pave the way for Jesus—to go before Him and help God's people get ready to receive His promised Savior and Rescuer. To do that, John used a simple message: repent. But repenting doesn't just mean to stop what you're doing; repentance is about turning. It's about turning from sin and disbelief and turning toward God's salvation and forgiveness. John preached this message faithfully, even to those who didn't want to hear they were living in disobedience, like the religious leaders of the time.

This is still an important message because all of us were born with hearts bent toward disbelief and sin. We must hear the same message, the message that shows us our sin and calls us to turn away from it. And when we do turn, we will find Jesus waiting to receive us with grace and forgiveness.

Reflect

1. Based on what we read, what do you think the strangest part of John's appearance was?

2. What was John's message, in your own words?

3. Why do we still need to hear that message?

Pray

Help us, Lord, not to be so prideful that we cannot recognize our own sin. Thank You for the chance to see our sin and turn from it to You.

 **Day 3**

The Ministry Begins

Show

If you are married, show the family your wedding ring and
ask them to tell you what it is and what it means. If you are not
married, then ask the family to tell you what they think it means to
be married, then explain that part of a marriage ceremony is the
exchanging of rings between the husband and wife. Explain that
the ring is a symbol of your marriage and commitment. Explain
that you got this ring at the beginning of the marriage—it was
the symbol of the beginning of a long journey. Then transition
to the next part of the story by explaining that in a similar way,
Jesus was going to begin a new phase of His life. And He had a
symbol that launched Him out as well.

Read

Matthew 3:13–17

Explain

The time had come. Jesus had spent some thirty years growing in wisdom and stature, but the time had come for God's
rescue plan, through Jesus, to go public. What had long been
planned in God's heart was about to be made visible for all to
see, and it started with baptism. John, though, was hesitant,
because John had been baptizing people as a symbol of their

repentance. Jesus, who had never sinned, had nothing to repent of. But this baptism for Jesus was not about repentance; it was about dedication. Jesus was showing everyone that He was completely committed to the will of His true Father, that He was giving His complete surrender to Him. When He came up from the water, the Father let everyone know that this was the Son, and He was doing the right thing. The Father was pleased with the Son.

Amazingly, when we believe in Jesus, we also become the sons and daughters of God. Because of Jesus' wholehearted commitment to obedience, the Father looks at us and says the same thing: "These are My children, and I am well pleased with them."

Reflect

1. Why was John hesitant to baptize Jesus?

2. Why was Jesus baptized?

3. How do we know Jesus did the right thing?

Pray

Thank You, Father, that You are pleased with Jesus. And thank You that because of Jesus, we can be Your children, too.

In the Desert

Show

Ask each family member when they get the hungriest during the day. Maybe it's mid-morning, middle of the afternoon, or right before bed. Then ask them what typically happens when they get hungry. While they might mention things like stomach pains, encourage them also to think beyond that to attitude changes like being irritable or short-tempered. Affirm that it's difficult to be hungry, but tell the family that Jesus understands everything about us, including what it feels like to be hungry, as you will see in the next part of the story.

Read

Matthew 4:1–11

Explain

The first step in the main part of God's rescue plan was a step into the wilderness, and that's where the Spirit of God led Jesus next. Once there, Jesus met an old enemy—one who was there in the garden. Jesus, for His part, had fasted for forty days and was hungry. But while we might think that Jesus was at His weakest, He had made Himself ready for the temptation from the devil. Three times the devil tempted Jesus, but three times Jesus withstood the temptation by trusting in the Word of God.

Unlike the first temptation, when Adam and Eve failed to trust in the Word of God, Jesus was stronger. Jesus succeeded where the first people had failed. He was tested. He was ready. As we follow Jesus, we can follow Him with confidence because we know He is more than strong enough to defeat His enemy and ours. But we also can see that the way to battle temptation in our own lives is the same way that Jesus did—by trusting in what we read in God's Word. Of course, we won't just know God's Word off the top of our heads unless we spend focused time reading and studying it—which is exactly what we should commit to doing.

Reflect

1. What happened to Jesus after He was baptized?

2. How did Jesus fight against temptation?

3. What are some of God's promises that will help us fight against temptation?

Pray

Lord, thank You for a strong Savior. Please help us to trust in Your Word as we see Jesus doing.

The Call

Show

Bring an umbrella with you to family devotion, and as the family gathers, extend the umbrella. See if you can put the entire family under it. Then explain that an umbrella is meant to protect us from rain. As long as you are under the umbrella, the rain should go off the umbrella and around you. But then also explain that sometimes people use the word *umbrella* to mean something that includes a lot of other things under it. For example, the term *cookie* could be an umbrella because oatmeal cookies, chocolate chip cookies, and snickerdoodles would all fit under that one term together. In a similar way, you will read some words Jesus spoke to a few men. These words of Jesus are an umbrella, both for them and for us.

Read

Matthew 4:18–22

Explain

Jesus was on a mission, but He wouldn't be going alone. He called others to go with Him, and that call came in the form of two simple words: "Follow Me." This is the same call that Jesus still issues to every man, woman, and child on earth. "Follow Me." Oh, certainly as we follow Jesus, He will tell us more things we need to do out of love and obedience, but everything else Jesus will command falls under the umbrella of those two words.

For these first disciples, following Jesus meant immediately leaving their old lives behind. They could not stay where they were, doing what they were doing, and follow Jesus at the same time. So it is with us. When Jesus calls us, He calls us to Him but also away from our old way of life. We may not have to move or change jobs, but we cannot keep living in the same way we have been.

Jesus also makes a promise along with His call. He promises that in following Him, we will find the true meaning of life and joy as we find our place in God's ongoing story.

Reflect

1. What was Jesus' call to these first disciples?

2. What did they have to leave behind to follow Jesus?

3. What are some of the things we have to leave behind if we want to follow Jesus?

Pray

You are calling us, Lord Jesus, to follow You. Help us not to look back at what we leave behind but instead keep our eyes fixed on You.

The First Sign

Show

As the family gathers, ask them to go around in a circle and share a type of sign they might see on the road. Examples include stop signs, speed limit signs, and yield signs. Keep going in a circle until no one can think of any more signs. Then explain that in today's story, you will see another kind of "sign." As you will see, this sign would reveal important information just like signs on the road. But the information in this case would be about who Jesus is and what He came to do.

Read

John 2:1–11

Explain

The hosts of the wedding had a problem. They had run out of wine, and in that time, this would have been very embarrassing. But Jesus' mother, Mary, knew her Son. And she knew that her Son could help. And He did. At the command of Jesus, the water was miraculously transformed into the finest sort of wine. But this miracle was not just for the sake of the guests at the wedding; this was a "sign." Signs show us things; they reveal important information to us. And in the book of John, Jesus' miracles are called "signs" because they are meant to reveal information about

His identity to us. We see from this sign the power of Jesus, but also the caring heart of Jesus who took action when He observed a need around Him. As a result, those who were following Him believed even more in Him.

We might look around us and see the "signs" of Jesus everywhere—we might see someone's heart being changed, we might see people helping others in Jesus' name, and we might see the good work of God as the good news is being shared. All these point us back to Jesus, reminding us that He is who He says He is, and He can do what He says He can do.

Reflect

1. What was the problem at the wedding?

2. How did Jesus help?

3. What does this sign show us about Jesus?

Pray

Jesus, You are indeed who You say You are. Help us to believe.

When Anger Is Good

Show

As the family gathers together for devotion, ask each person to give you their best angry face. Allow each person to present a face before the group, then transition to the next part of the story. Explain that we often think about Jesus as being kind, compassionate, and loving. He is certainly all those things, but in the next part of the story, we will see a different side of Jesus.

Read

John 2:13–22

Explain

What could make Jesus, the Son of God who is rich in mercy, love, and grace, behave this way? It was when He saw how the temple of God was being treated. The temple was meant to be a place of honor, sacrifice, and prayer—a place in which God's people could come and meet with Him. But by this time, the temple had become a money-making destination, a place where merchants and the people bought and sold the sacrifices they were to make. Seeing how the temple had been changed, Jesus was filled with anger.

But this anger was not an example of Jesus losing His temper; no, this was a righteous anger. People were being taken advantage of rather than welcomed to pray and meet with God. But Jesus also knew something that the disciples did not—there was a greater temple than the one they were in. Jesus Himself is the temple—it is through Jesus that people can truly meet with and encounter God. And Jesus knew that this temple would be destroyed, but not permanently. Jesus would die, but then three days later, would rise again. In this way, the "temple" would be destroyed and be rebuilt. The disciples did not yet understand what Jesus meant by this, but in time, they would.

Reflect

1. Why was Jesus so angry?

2. What was the other "temple" Jesus was talking about?

3. What would happen to this "temple"?

Pray

Jesus, thank You that in You we can freely come to God and be received as His children.

A Visit at Night

Show

To begin today's family devotion, ask each family member to share one person from history they would like to have a conversation with and why. Explain that we might have all kinds of questions for these historical people—questions about their lives, their circumstances, and their achievements. Transition to the next part of the story by saying that as important as all these questions are, there is an even more important issue. This is the issue we see being brought to Jesus in the next part of the story.

Read

John 3:16–21

Explain

Nicodemus was a Pharisee, one of the religious leaders of Jesus' time. While most Pharisees were suspicious of Jesus, Nicodemus knew there was something different about Him. But Nicodemus was also afraid of how it would look for him, a Pharisee, to be seen asking Jesus questions. After all, Nicodemus was one of the people who was supposed to know all the answers, not have more questions. So he came to Jesus at night, when he wouldn't be seen, to talk to Jesus about who He really is, and the way to eternal life. And Jesus was more than happy to give the answer.

As Jesus explained to Nicodemus, no one can really come into the kingdom of God and become God's children unless they are born again. We have seen, in our story, this same message time and time again. All of us are sinful, and all of us need new hearts. New life. New birth. We need to be made new by believing in Jesus. And whosoever does believe in Jesus can be made new.

Reflect

1. Who was Nicodemus and why did he come to Jesus at night?

2. What did Nicodemus want to talk to Jesus about?

3. What is the message Jesus shared with Nicodemus?

Pray

Thank You, Lord, that by believing in Jesus we can be born again. Help us to do just that—to trust in Jesus for forgiveness and new birth.

Living Water

Show

Prior to family devotion, place several cups of water and straws at one end of the room or yard, and a larger cup at the other end. Explain to the family that you will play a water-cup-filling game. Each family member will use their own cup, and suck water into a straw and then have to transfer it to the larger cup. You will work together, seeing how quickly you can fill the larger cup. You might play a couple of times to see if you can improve on your time, then gather your family together and transition to the devotion. Explain that in the days of Jesus, people had to draw water from a well, maybe a few times a day, and move it to their homes to use. But as you will see today, Jesus offers us a greater kind of water. This water is more important than water we can get from a well or a faucet.

Read

John 4:13–26

Explain

The conversation was an unusual one. Jews and Samaritans did not get along with each other, and men did not often talk to women one on one. So it was unusual that Jesus, a Jewish man, would engage this Samaritan woman in conversation—but that's exactly what He did. While they began talking about the well and the water, Jesus shifted the conversation to something more important. According to Jesus, He could give this woman living water—it was water for the heart and soul, not water to drink. According to Jesus, both Jews and Samaritans, with all their differences, need this water. In fact, once you drink of this water, you will never be thirsty again.

Like this Samaritan woman, we are all sinful, and in our sin, we are thirsty for something more than the world can offer. It's only through Jesus that our hearts and souls can be quenched.

Reflect

1. Why was it unusual for Jesus and this woman to have a conversation?

2. What's different about the kind of water Jesus is offering?

3. Why do we need this living water?

Pray

Jesus, thank You that You are the fountain of living water. Help us to drink deeply from what only You can provide.

Walking Away

Show

As the family gathers together, explain that you want to take them on a journey back in time thirty-eight years earlier. Then tell them some facts about what was going on thirty-eight years ago—a significant news story, the number one movie or song, or maybe a popular athlete or celebrity. Transition to today's part of the story by explaining that though a lot can happen in thirty-eight years, you will meet a man today whose life had been pretty much the same for that amount of time.

Read

John 5:2–9

Explain

The man was laying by a famous pool in Jerusalem, and he was not alone. Many other people who were sick and disabled stayed there every day because of a legend. The story went that every once in a while, an angel would come and stir the waters in the pool, and if you were quick enough to get into it, then you would be healed. For this man, the healing was a long time in coming—he had been disabled for thirty-eight years. He had, it seems, put all his hope in this legend, waiting for the pool to be stirred and then hoping to get into it.

But Jesus is no legend. He is no myth or fairy tale. He showed the man that He had the true power. Jesus healed the man, and the man got up and walked away for the first time in almost four decades. But there was a problem—Jesus did this on the Sabbath, and many of the religious leaders were angry about it. But Jesus knew the true meaning of the Sabbath. It was not just a break from work, but instead a chance to remember, celebrate, and honor God for what He had done. It was right for Jesus to heal this man then because Jesus was doing the will of His Father. Jesus took notice of this man who everyone else had forgotten. We, too, might feel forgotten sometimes, but we can know that Jesus takes notice of us as well.

Reflect

1. Why was this man laying by this pool?

2. What did Jesus show the man about Himself?

3. Why were people mad at Jesus for this healing?

Pray

Jesus, help us remember that You are real instead of some legend. Thank You that You will always take notice of those in need.

 **Day 3**

Homecoming

Show

To begin today's family devotion, share a story about a time when you went back to your hometown for an event. It might be for a homecoming football game, a family reunion, or a class reunion. Share what you did, how things were different, and what . the celebrations were like. Explain that we often do things like this—provide opportunities to come back home, and opportunities like that are usually chances for people to share with each other what their lives have been like since they left. Transition to the next part of the story—a homecoming for Jesus. But it didn't end like you might expect.

Read

Luke 4:16–28

Explain

Jesus had been making a name for Himself, both in His teaching and in the miracles He was performing. No doubt His hometown of Nazareth was excited to have Him visit, and Jesus did not disappoint. He went into their place of worship, opened the scroll, and read a prophecy about the Messiah. Then He told the people that the time for the Messiah had come—and it was Him!

Now we might expect the people to be excited—even thrilled—that the Rescuer had come, and He had come from their town. The people were, until Jesus continued on. He went on to explain to the people that they were wrong in thinking that the Rescuer had come just for them. He was not coming to help and save the Jewish people only, but all different kinds of people. This was definitely not what they expected, but this was the mission of Jesus. In fact, Jesus was such a different kind of Messiah that they even drove Him to the edge of the hill to try and kill Him. But in His power, Jesus walked right through them.

We can be thankful today that Jesus was not the Savior that everyone expected. We can rejoice that Jesus is the Savior of the entire world.

Reflect

1. Why were the people excited at first?

2. Why did they then get so angry with Jesus?

3. Why should this part of the story make us thankful?

Pray

Thank You, Jesus, that You did not just come to save a few, but to save anyone who comes to You in faith.

True Blessing

Show

As the family gathers together, ask for a volunteer to read from the Bible. But as you hand the Bible to the volunteer, turn it upside down and challenge them to see if they can read it. Give a few more family members the same challenge, then use the exercise to transition into the next part of the story. Explain that the people of Jesus' day thought they knew what it meant to be blessed. But Jesus, in His teaching, told them the truth, and He turned everything upside down.

Read

Matthew 5:1–12

Explain

What does it mean to be blessed? The people of Jesus' day thought they knew. To be blessed meant to have plenty of food, to be wealthy, and to have no sickness or pain in their lives. But Jesus flipped that understanding on its head. Jesus is teaching us that life in the kingdom of God is very different than life in the kingdom of the world. It's the people the world looks at as not being blessed that are considered blessed in God's kingdom. That's because all these things—money, health, prosperity—that we think of as being blessings can often put up barriers between us and God. For those who have very little on earth, it can be easier to put their faith in and find their happiness only in God.

We should be careful to remember, if we are Christians, that there is much more for us than what this earth has to offer. We should make sure that we are never putting our faith, trust, and happiness in the things of this world and instead in Jesus alone.

Reflect

1. What is most surprising to you about this teaching from Jesus?

2. How does this teaching show us the difference between the kingdom of God and the kingdom of this world?

3. Why does Jesus call these people blessed?

Pray

Lord, help us not to put our faith in anything except You. Help us to find our joy and satisfaction in You alone.

Fulfilling the Law

Show

Explain that to start the family devotion today, you are going to have a little history lesson. For centuries, mankind believed Earth was at the center of the solar system, and that the sun and all the stars revolved around Earth. It wasn't until the sixteenth century that Nicolas Copernicus developed a model with the sun at the center. Many people didn't like it because the model forced people to think that maybe they, and their planet, weren't at the center of everything. Jesus does something similar for us spiritually. He is the center of all things, even our own stories. As we see Jesus continue His teaching today, we will see Him describing Himself this way.

Read

Matthew 5:17–20

Explain

There was a growing misunderstanding of Jesus. Because He did things like heal people on the Sabbath, and because He challenged the way the religious leaders understood the law, people thought Jesus came to throw the law away and start over. But this is not so. If it was, it would mean that God made a mistake in giving His people the law to begin with. No, Jesus did not come to throw away the law; He came to fulfill the law. See, only someone who lived perfectly in heart as well as obedience could fulfill the law. And only Jesus is able to do that. We cannot, just as the people of His day could not. But when we trust in Jesus, we can receive His righteousness. Jesus takes all our sin and the punishment for it on Him, and we get the reward of His perfect life.

Reflect

1. Why did people think Jesus was throwing away the law?

2. In what way was Jesus fulfilling the law?

3. How can our righteousness surpass that of the Pharisees?

Pray

Jesus, thank You for living the perfect life. Thank You for being willing to exchange Your perfect life for our sinful ones.

How to Pray

Show

Explain to the family that you are going to create a simple, dot-to-dot picture together. Ask for some suggestions of the image you are going to create, then begin dotting out the outline of the picture. Number each of the dots in the order they are to be connected. Ask for a volunteer to complete the picture, then ask the family what makes a dot-to-dot picture successful. Of course, the only way the picture works is if the person completing the picture follows the numbers perfectly. One mistake causes the picture to become skewed. Transition to the next part of the story, telling the family that sometimes we think prayer works like that—there is a certain recipe we have to follow perfectly or otherwise it doesn't work. But as you will see today, Jesus didn't teach us a specific prayer, like completing a dot-to-dot, but instead taught us how to pray.

Read

Matthew 6:9–13

Explain

The disciples came to Jesus with a question, and it was a question He was more than happy to answer. They wanted to know how to pray. In response, Jesus didn't give them the exact words to pray, but instead demonstrated the kinds of things they should be praying about.

This model prayer starts with an understanding that God is our Father, and that should be very comforting to us indeed. When we pray, we aren't talking to a distant God, but to the One who has brought us into His family, adopted us as His children. All our prayers should be done for our Father's glory, so people everywhere might know and honor His name and that His kingdom would be advanced. But that doesn't mean we also shouldn't pray about the very specific things we need; we certainly should. Like any good father, God wants to provide for us in the right way and at the right time. And because God is our Father, we can also trust He will forgive us when we confess our sins to Him. Once again, we know all this to be true and right when God is our Father, but God only becomes our Father when we put our faith in Jesus alone. It's only through Him that we have the open door to God in prayer.

Reflect

1. What is the difference between knowing how to pray, and knowing what to pray?

2. How does knowing God is our Father help us pray?

3. What is one way we can spend more time praying throughout the day?

Pray

Father, thank You that You are great, and that You also care so much about us and our needs. Help us to come to You quickly and confidently in prayer.

True Authority

Show

To begin today's family devotion, explain that you are going to talk about authority. Explain that to have authority over someone means you have the right to tell them what to do. To illustrate this, ask the family who is one person who has authority over them. Then ask them to trace the line of authority back. Who has authority over that person, then the next person, and so on. Do this several times, establishing the fact that in most areas of life, there is a line of authority. Explain that the subject is important for the next part of the story, because we see that there was at least one person who understood the authority Jesus possesses.

Read

Matthew 8:5–13

Explain

As Jesus entered a new city in His travels, He encountered an important soldier. This man would have commanded many people in the Roman army, but He also was compassionate. His servant was sick, and He had come to ask Jesus to heal the servant. Though Jesus was willing to go with the man to heal the servant, the man knew something about authority. He knew that Jesus did not have to be present to heal the servant; Jesus had authority over life and death. All Jesus had to do was order it to be done, and it would be done.

This is true faith—believing that Jesus can do what He claims He can do. And this faith was amazing to Jesus. He was never amazed by the faith of those who were following Him most closely, but this man, who had very little knowledge of Jesus or the Jewish people, knew enough. For us, true faith is really this simple. It is recognizing the authority of Jesus, and then taking Him at His Word, believing He can do what He says He can do.

Reflect

1. Who was the man who came to Jesus?

2. How did the man show faith in Jesus?

3. How can this encounter help us understand what faith is?

Pray

Lord, help us not to overcomplicate believing in You. Help us to read Your Word, and believe You are who you say You are and can do what You say You can do.

Dealing with Doubt

Show

Distribute pens, paper, and crayons or colored pencils to the family. Ask them to take about a minute each, and draw a picture of a sign they have seen in the last twenty-four hours. After the minute, allow each family member to show their sign, explain where they saw it, and tell what it means. Remind the family that in a previous devotion, you discussed that signs are meant to communicate information that we need to know. Also remind the family that Jesus' miracles are called "signs" in the Bible because they are meant to communicate information about Him and His mission. Explain that in the next part of the story, we will see someone who needed some information because he was doubting what he thought was true.

Read

Matthew 11:1–6

Explain

If anyone knew the identity and mission of Jesus, you would think it would be John the Baptist. After all, he paved the way for Jesus with his preaching. But John the Baptist had been arrested when he refused to be silent about sin in the house of the ruler of the land, and in prison, John was quite sure he was going to be put to death. And in his jail cell, he had begun to wonder if he might have been wrong about Jesus.

Like John, we too might be in difficult or painful circumstances. And in those circumstances we too might wonder if Jesus really is who He said He is and can do what He said He could do. So John did just the right thing with His doubt. Rather than hide it, he took it straight to Jesus. In response, Jesus said that John should look to the signs that accompanied Jesus. But these weren't only signs—they were prophecies from the Bible that Jesus was fulfilling. When we have doubts about God, we should do the same thing. We should pray about them, then we should look back to the Bible and trust what it says to be true about God. From time to time, most of us will have doubts, but even in our doubts, God is merciful and will help us through His Word.

Reflect

1. What happened to John?

2. What did Jesus say that John should do when he doubted?

3. How can this help us know what to do when we have doubts?

Pray

We are weak and frail, Lord. Thank You for helping us even in our doubts.

The Farmer and the Kingdom

Show

Prior to the devotion, gather together four clear cups, each filled with a different substance. Fill one with dirt, but fill the others with things like rocks, blocks, marbles, water, etc. Present the cups before the family, and ask them if they were going to plant a seed, which cup they would plant it in. Explain that Jesus often told stories when He was speaking to people, and those people received His teaching in all kinds of ways. You might say that the hearts of people were like the cups. One story in particular was about planting seeds, and this story shows us why Jesus told all His other stories.

Read

Matthew 13:1–13

Explain

The story was a simple one. A farmer spread the same seed out on different kinds of ground. But what happened next depended on the kind of ground the seed fell on. In Jesus' story, the seed represents His words. Jesus preached to and taught all kinds of people. Some of them believed in Him, some did not, and some only believed for a short time. This is how the message of God's kingdom worked, and it's also why Jesus spoke in stories

329

like this called parables. Those whose hearts were like good soil were ready to receive His teaching. Because they believed in Him, they were able to receive, understand, and obey His words. But many others had hearts that were like other kinds of soil, and though the seed was good, it did not grow and bear fruit because the soil was bad.

One of the ways God works in us is by preparing our hearts to receive the words of Jesus. We should be praying not only for our hearts, but also for the hearts of those around us, that they would be like good soil, fertile ground that will bear much gospel fruit.

Reflect

1. Retell Jesus' story in your own words.

2. What does the seed represent? What does the soil represent?

3. How should we respond to the parable of the sower?

Pray

Jesus, please make our hearts good soil for Your word. We also pray that You would go before us and make good soil of the hearts of those we have the chance to speak to about You.

A Miracle on the Way

Show

When the family is gathered together, explain that you will begin today with each person taking their own pulse. Explain that your pulse is the rate at which your heart is beating. You can measure your pulse by putting two fingers on your neck, just to the side of your throat. Demonstrate how to do this, then ask each person to take their pulse. Explain that when you go to the doctor, one of the first things the doctor does is take your vital signs. This includes things like your pulse and blood pressure. These are the first indicators of whether you are in quick need of medical treatment. Transition to today's part of the story by saying that you will see someone who was in desperate need of help, and so that person's family came to Jesus.

Read

Mark 5:21–42

Explain

Jairus did exactly the right thing. His daughter was dangerously sick, and he came straight to Jesus for help. This is what we should do any time we need help. Prayer ought to be the first place we turn, and we will find Jesus waiting to help us just as He did with Jairus.

On His way to help the little girl, Jesus was interrupted by a woman who also needed help. But she was not so bold as to come to Him directly; instead, she believed if she could only touch His clothing she would be healed. Jesus, rather than being annoyed by the interruption, healed this woman. This should be of great comfort to us because it means that we are never bothering Jesus. He's never too busy to listen to our prayers.

Unfortunately, though, in the time it took Jesus to interact with this woman, the little girl had died. But even death is no match for Jesus. Indeed, this was the reason He had come—to defeat death for all who believe in Him. And that's what He did for this little girl. Jesus is the Rescuer who, though He came to defeat sin and death, is not too busy for any of our needs.

Reflect

1. How was Jesus interrupted on His way to help Jairus's daughter?

2. What does this show us about Jesus?

3. Why is it important that we remember what happened to Jairus's daughter?

Pray

Jesus, You are the Lord of everything—even death. Thank You that even though You are great, You are not too busy for any of us.

More Than Enough

Show

Present one small piece of candy before the family. Explain that you want everyone to have some candy, so you are going to try and divide the piece of candy evenly for everyone. Make a show of trying to measure it out and cut it. Then explain that there is a far simpler solution if you want everyone to have candy—just get more. Use this to transition into the next part of the story, explaining that one day Jesus was teaching up until dinner time. But there was a very small amount of food there, and with such a small amount, the disciples didn't know what to do. But Jesus did.

Read

John 6:1–14

Explain

The crowd was large, and the hour was late. The disciples wanted to be able to provide food for the huge amount of people, but the supplies and the money were short. In fact, the only resources they had came from a small boy who volunteered his fish and bread to be able to help. Despite the seemingly impossible situation, it was really only this boy who did the right thing—he took what he had, offered it to Jesus, and let Jesus do the rest. From this small offering, Jesus performed yet another miracle, providing enough food for all the people. In fact, Jesus provided more than enough—there were twelve basketfuls left over, one for each disciple, to remind them that Jesus always abundantly provides.

When we feel overwhelmed because we don't feel like we are smart enough, tough enough, or resourceful enough in the face of our circumstances, we can learn much from the boy in this story. In faith, we can bring what we have to Jesus and trust Him to make much out of our weakness.

Reflect

1. What was the problem the disciples faced?

2. How were the responses of the disciples and the little boy different?

3. What can we learn from this little boy?

Pray

Jesus, thank You that You don't just provide, but provide abundantly. Help us to offer You what resources we have and trust You to do the rest.

Week 40 Day 4

Lost and Found

Show

Before family devotion, gather together paper, pens, and colored pencils or crayons. Ask the family to imagine that they have a pet who is lost, or if you have a pet, ask them to imagine that your pet is lost. Then ask them to create a poster you might hang up in the neighborhood in order to help find him or her. Explain that in the next part of the story, you will hear Jesus tell a story about something that was lost, then found, then celebrated.

Read

Luke 15:4–7

Explain

In Jesus' story, one of the sheep was lost. Perhaps the man who owned the sheep might have thought, *I still have 99 sheep; it's not that big of a deal that I've lost one.* But that would not be the attitude of a good shepherd. And the shepherd in Jesus' story was a good one. This shepherd struck out to find the sheep rather than waiting and hoping the sheep would come home. And when he found him, the shepherd threw the sheep on his back and carried him home. And if that wasn't enough, there was a huge celebration when the sheep was returned.

The point of Jesus' story was to show us just how intent God is on rescuing people He loves. He did not wait for people to come to Him, but instead sent His own Son, the Good Shepherd, to seek out those who were lost and bring them home. Jesus is still seeking sinners out, and every time He brings one back into right relationship with God, there is a huge heavenly celebration. This is how much God values each and every person. This is how much each and every person matters.

Reflect

1. Summarize Jesus' story in your own words.

2. Why do you think Jesus told this story?

3. What does this story teach us about God?

Pray

Jesus, You are the Good Shepherd. Thank You for not leaving us when we were lost but instead coming to find us.

Walking on Water

Show

To prepare for family devotion, gather together a large bowl filled with water and several small objects of different substance (i.e., pencil, rock, piece of fruit, etc.). For each object, the family will vote on the question of whether it will float or not. Go through each object, voting on each one, and then testing it out. After you have tested all the other objects, ask what would happen if one of you stepped into the bowl of water. Obviously, you would not float. But then transition to the next portion of the study, by saying that in His next miracle, Jesus didn't just make someone float—He actually walked—and made someone else walk—on the water.

Read

Matthew 14:22–33

Explain

Jesus has power over diseases. He has power over demons. He even has power over death. But His disciples learned He also has power over nature. Despite the powerful storm on the sea, Jesus was calmly strolling on top of the water toward the disciples. The disciples were amazed—even terrified—but Peter believed. In fact, he was so confident in Jesus that he asked Jesus to call him out on the water too. First one step, then another—Peter found himself walking toward Jesus. But after just a few steps, Peter took his eyes off Jesus and started focusing on the wind and waves around him. He lost focus, and he began to sink. But even in his loss of focus, Jesus was more than powerful enough to reach down and save him.

There is a powerful truth in this part of the story for us. When we are walking with Jesus, our main priority is to keep our eyes focused on Him. We have the tendency to remove our focus from Jesus and start focusing on our circumstances around us, but when we do, we will find ourselves sinking under those circumstances. Fortunately, even when that happens, Jesus stands ready to give us His strength even in our weakness.

Reflect

1. What was the miracle that Jesus performed?

2. How did Peter respond?

3. What can we learn about the importance of keeping our focus on Jesus?

Pray

Lord, our hearts and our focus tend to wander from You. Help us to keep our eyes firmly fixed on You and You alone.

Confession and Prediction

Show

As the family gathers together, ask them if they know the name Albert Einstein. Though most people would know the name, in case they do not, briefly explain that Einstein is generally regarded as one of the greatest scientists and thinkers of the last hundred years. Then ask the family if they are familiar with Einstein's most famous theory—the theory of relativity (E equals MC squared). Hopefully, someone will know that answer, but then ask the person to explain it. Though they might know the answer, they might not know exactly what it means. This is kind of like what you will see happening next in the story. Jesus asked His disciples a very important question, and though Peter got the answer right, he did not yet understand all of what it meant.

Read

Luke 9:18–22

Explain

Jesus had an important question. In fact, it was the most important question. This is the question that every man, woman, and child must answer in their lives: "Who do you say that I am?" This is a personal question. It's not a question that parents can answer for their children, or children can answer for their parents. It's for each person to answer themselves.

In this case, Peter knew the right answer. It's true, Jesus was and is God's Messiah—the Savior that had come into the world. But Peter, along with the rest of the disciples, did not understand the full meaning of this. Peter was still thinking that Jesus was the kind of savior who would lead an army and do battle against the Romans. But He is instead the kind of Savior who does battle against sin and death, and would win victory not through a battle but through His death on the cross.

It's important that we recognize this, just as Peter needed to. We must embrace Jesus as the true Savior, not as some other savior we think we need. So the question from Jesus comes again to us today, and every day: "Who do you say that I am?"

Reflect

1. What is the important question Jesus asked?

2. Why was Peter's answer right and wrong at the same time?

3. Why must we answer this question for ourselves?

Pray

Jesus, You are the Messiah. Thank You that You won the right kind of victory over the right enemy.

A Visit from Friends

Show

As the family gathers together, invite each person to share their favorite specific memory from a family vacation you have taken together. Allow each person to share their memory, and then ask if anyone has ever thought about staying on vacation forever. Chances are, at least one member of the family will say yes, that they wish you could indeed stay on vacation forever. But remind them that even though we might enjoy times like these, we always have to return to the lives God intended us to live. Transition to the next part of the story by saying that, like us, Jesus' disciples had a moment they wished they could stay in. But Jesus helped them see that they, too, were meant to live in real life.

Read

Luke 9:28–36

Explain

It was a remarkable sight. Peter, James, and John witnessed Jesus transformed before their eyes. And not only Jesus, but Moses and Elijah were there as well! The three were having a conversation before their eyes, but what would these three talk about? They were talking about Jesus' departure, and both Moses and Elijah knew something about departures. Moses led the Israelites on a departure from Egypt; Elijah departed from the earth in a whirlwind; and soon Jesus would both depart and lead a departure with Him. He would lead people from every background on a departure from sin and death, and He would eventually be taken up into heaven Himself.

The sight was so amazing that Peter wanted to stay there, to build homes and shelters and stay on the mountain. But Jesus knew it was not to be. He had a mission, and the disciples would have a mission as well. Their mission had to be lived out in the real world.

Reflect

1. What did Peter, James, and John see on the mountain?

2. What were the three talking about?

3. Why is it important for us to remember that we cannot stay on top of the mountain?

Pray

Lord, thank You for the departure You are leading. Help us to remember our place in that mission and to embrace it.

Good Neighbors

Show

Walk the family outside to begin the family devotion, and say the names and a little information about as many of your neighbors as you are able. Explain that in devotion today you will see Jesus telling a story about neighbors as well, though the way Jesus described neighbors was surprising to the person He was talking to.

Read

Luke 10:25–37

Explain

Some questions are good questions. We ask good questions when we are truly curious or interested in learning the answer. But the man who asked Jesus this question was not interested in either one. Instead, he wanted to try and make Jesus say something wrong, or something that would get Him in trouble. Even so, Jesus answered his question and told the man the two most important things in life: to love God, and to love our neighbors. And to show the man that a person's neighbors are more than just the people around him. Jesus told him the story of a man who was willing to go out of his way to help someone he didn't know and at his own expense. To top it off, this good neighbor was a Samaritan!

It's a powerful story, and a powerful reminder to us, that we do not pick and choose who our neighbors are. Our neighbors are the people God chooses to put in our paths. And it's God's will that we are active in helping them, even if they're people we wouldn't naturally want to help, and even if it means some cost to us. We do this because we know that long before we help someone else, God has done even more for us. For we all were dying in our own sin, but God crossed the divide between earth and heaven and gave His only Son to help us.

Reflect

1. Why did the man ask Jesus these questions?

2. What part of Jesus' story sticks out the most to you?

3. Who is one person in your life who needs help right now, and how can you help that person?

Pray

Lord, thank You that You are the greatest neighbor. Help us to love others in the way that You have loved us.

 **Week 42** **Day 1**

A Special Guest

Show

Ask the family to imagine that you were going to host the mayor of your town or city tonight in your home for dinner, and then make a list together of everything you would want to accomplish before he or she arrived. No doubt you would want to make sure the house was clean, a special dessert was made, or the right music was picked out. We would want to do those things because the guest would be very special, and we would want them to feel special and honored in our home. Explain to the family that in the next part of the story, you will see Jesus coming to dinner with a family, and in the same way, the family wanted everything to be just right. But Jesus wanted them to know He had something different in mind.

Read

Luke 10:38–42

Explain

Martha wanted everything to be just right for Jesus. She busied herself with all the household tasks, while her sister, Mary, simply sat and listened to Jesus. Martha was getting frustrated with her sister, but Jesus helped Martha see the true priority. For

345

Jesus, it was more important that Martha was with Him than it was that she serve Him.

Isn't it amazing to think that Jesus actually wants to spend time with us? He doesn't just want us to obey His orders, like He's some general; rather, He wants us to sit with Him. To learn from Him. To love being with Him. The Bible calls time like this when we sit, read the Bible, pray, and reflect "abiding." And this is the main practice we need to have as we follow Jesus—to abide with Him. Unfortunately, many times we get too busy or distracted, and fail to spend time with Jesus. But He is always ready to spend time with us. We must be careful to keep first things first, and time with Jesus should always come first.

Reflect

1. What did Jesus teach Mary and Martha?

2. What are some of the reasons we might not be spending time with Jesus?

3. What is one way you can plan to spend more time with Jesus each day?

Pray

Jesus, thank You that You actually desire to spend time with us. Help us to grow in our desire to spend time with You.

Give It Away

Show

After the family has gathered, ask each family member to go back to their rooms and get one article of clothing they would like to give away to someone else. When everyone returns, ask each person to show which article they chose. After everyone has had a chance to do so, ask if anyone chose their favorite shirt, pair of shoes, etc. Chances are, no one will have done so. The point of the illustration is not to shame the family for not choosing a favorite item, but just to point out that we are typically more ready to give things away that we don't really want anymore. Then ask the family to imagine being told not just to give away one article of clothing, but instead everything they have. This is what you will see happening in the next part of the story.

Read

Mark 10:17–22

Explain

The young man was desperate. He had everything that everyone thought would make him happy and complete. He was young, he was rich, and he was powerful, and yet something was lacking in his life. He came to Jesus asking for the answer to what was missing: "What must I do to inherit eternal life?" Before

He responded, Jesus looked at the young man and loved him. This is very important, because it means that whatever Jesus told the young man to do next came out of His great love. At first, Jesus told the young man that he should keep the commandments, and the man claimed to have done just that (though he surely had not, at least not perfectly). So Jesus went straight to the heart of the matter. He looked at the young man and knew what was holding him back—this man loved his possessions more than anything. In order to have eternal life, the man had to release what was holding his heart hostage and instead trust in Jesus to fill in what was lacking.

Like this man, we all tend to have something or someone that we are using to try and make us feel complete. And Jesus would say the same thing to us. He might not tell us to sell our possessions, but He will tell us to give up that which we are using to fill us up in the way only Jesus can. Jesus must be our treasure. He must be what we love most. Until He is, we will never really be joyful and satisfied.

Reflect

1. What was the young man's problem?
2. What did Jesus tell him to do?
3. Why would Jesus tell him to do that?

Pray

Help us, Lord, to know if there is something we are treasuring more than You. Help us have the courage and the strength to trust and love You first.

A Wee Little Man

Show

Walk the family outside, and ask each person to pick a tree they would most like to climb. In turn, ask each one to share which tree they chose and why. Then explain that when Jesus was traveling through the land, most everyone wanted to see Him. Sometimes that meant people had to go to great lengths to do so. And in the next portion of the story, you will meet a man from Jericho who was even willing to climb up a tree in order to see Jesus.

Read

Luke 19:1–9

Explain

Zacchaeus wanted to see Jesus. Problem was, he was very short, and the crowd was very thick. The only way Zacchaeus would be able to see Jesus was to climb up a tree close to the back of the crowd, and that would be fine with him. See, Zacchaeus wasn't really welcome among the people because he was a tax collector. He was the kind of person who worked for the Roman government even though he was Jewish, so many people thought of him as a traitor. Imagine his surprise, then, when Jesus was walking along the road and looked straight up into the tree. It seems that as much as Zacchaeus wanted to see Jesus, Jesus wanted to see Zacchaeus even more. In fact, Jesus even said that He had to stay at Zacchaeus' house that very day, and that's just what He did. When no one else wanted to be around Zacchaeus, Jesus was not only willing to talk to him, but to actually go to his house.

This is actually one of the reasons people were so mad at Jesus—He was willing to be friends with the people no one else would. But according to Jesus, this was the whole reason He came. He came to seek out and to save the lost, and that's just who Zacchaeus was. But not anymore. When he met Jesus, his life was forever and dramatically changed. Zacchaeus not only believed in Jesus, but he demonstrated that belief in real ways like giving back all the money he had unfairly collected from others and more. The same thing happens to us. We might not have many friends, we might feel like we are on the outside, we might feel lost in life, but Jesus is never too busy for us. He wants to meet us and spend time with us, and when He does, our lives will be changed.

Reflect

1. Who was Zacchaeus, and what did people think of him?

2. What did Jesus think of him? How do you know?

3. How does this part of the story show us Jesus' mission?

Pray

Thank You, Jesus, that You are a friend to those who don't have any. Thank You that You are willing to do what no one else would, and love who no one else would.

Power over the Grave

Show

Prior to family devotion, clip a small branch from a tree and bring it with you. Show the branch to the family, and then ask them how you can keep the branch alive. Suggest that maybe you could put it in some water, or bury part of it in the dirt, or leave it in the sunlight. Point out that none of these things would work because the branch is actually already dead. Once something is dead, we do not have any power to change that. But remind the family that Jesus is the One who has power over death, and point out that as the story continues, you are going to see Him exercise that power in an undeniable way. Explain that prior to reading from the Bible, there are some details the family needs to know. The same sisters you met a few days ago had a brother named Lazarus who became very sick. Because they were friends of Jesus, and because they knew Jesus could help, they sent word to Him to come. But then Jesus did something surprising—He waited where He was, and in the time He was waiting, Lazarus died. But the Bible tells us that Jesus waited purposely, not because He didn't care about Lazarus, Mary, or Martha, but so that God's power and glory would be made known.

Read

John 11:38–44

Explain

Jesus walked into a hopeless situation. Though He might have come sooner, He delayed, and now there was no doubt whatsoever that Lazarus was dead. In fact, he had already been in the tomb for four days. But Jesus was about to show that there was no limit to His power. Death had come into the world as the punishment for sin, and Jesus had come to reverse that curse, delivering those who believe in Him from both sin and death. As a sign of His power and what was to come, Jesus boldly prayed and then issued a command to Lazarus, and His dead friend responded to the authority of Jesus. Death could not hold him because Jesus had set him free.

Soon, Jesus Himself would be buried in a tomb, and once again, God's power and glory would be displayed as Jesus Himself would come forth from His own tomb. When we trust in Him, we can know that even when our bodies die, we will never really experience the true, spiritual death that is the punishment for sin. And, like Lazarus and Jesus, one day our dead bodies will come out of the grave, and we will be made to live forever. Jesus came to bring life, and He offers that life to any who believe.

Reflect

1. Why did Jesus wait to go and help Lazarus?

2. What does this part of the story show us about Jesus and His mission?

3. What can we know for sure if we believe in Jesus?

Pray

Jesus, Your power is immeasurable. Even the grave cannot stop You. Thank You that You bring life from death.

Into the City

Show

Ask each family member to share one of their favorite traditions that you have as a family. It might be a tradition around a holiday, the way you celebrate birthdays, or something that happens on the first day of school. Let every person share their favorite, then encourage the family by explaining that traditions are important because they help us remember things. People have always had traditions, even in the Bible. The Passover had become a tradition for God's people, a time to eat and drink special things and to come to Jerusalem so they would remember how God saved them from the Egyptians hundreds of years earlier. Jesus, too, was going to Jerusalem; but He was going for a different reason than anyone else.

Read

Matthew 21:1–11

Explain

There were many, many people in Jerusalem just like there were every year during the Passover. But this year, the people were trying to honor and welcome Jesus; that's why they were putting their coats on the ground and waving palm branches. But even though the people meant well, this was not the proper way to welcome a king. A king would not be riding a donkey. The road would not be lined with palm branches and coats. In that day, a king would be riding a great stallion and would be showered with things like gold. But Jesus is not that kind of king. He wasn't born as you would think a king should be born; He didn't live as you would think a king would live; and soon, He would die like you would not expect a king to die.

Jesus is altogether different, a King who rules through love, grace, and service. All of this was just as it should be; it was just as God had been planning since the very beginning. The King was in Jerusalem. And His time was drawing short.

Reflect

1. Why were there so many people in Jerusalem?

2. What was strange about the way Jesus was welcomed there?

3. What are some ways we might honor Jesus today?

Pray

Jesus, thank You that You are indeed a different kind of King. Help us to live in such a way that honors You and recognizes what You have done for us.

Washing Feet

Show

Challenge the family to a "dirty clothes" contest. Each family member will take one minute, go to their room, and find the dirtiest piece of clothing there. Once they bring it back, make a show of inspecting each one, looking it over and smelling it, then declare a winner. Transition to the next part of the story by saying that as dirty as these clothes are, they are probably not as dirty as what we would have seen in Jesus' day. People walked everywhere, and it was dirty and dusty on the roads. People's feet, then, were extremely dirty because they wore sandals. Ask the family to try and remember that as you read the next part of the story.

Read

John 13:1–17

Explain

Jesus, the unlikely King who entered on a donkey, knelt with a basin of water beside Him and washed the feet of His friends. With each foot, the water became more and more nasty, a reminder of just how dirty the job was. Peter was appalled because he didn't feel like Jesus should be lowering Himself to the level of doing this. But Jesus reminded Peter that if Jesus didn't wash

Peter then Peter would have no part with Him. The same thing is true with us, except that Jesus doesn't just wash our feet; He washes our hearts clean from sin. If He doesn't do that, then we have no part with Him.

In this act, Jesus was showing us His willingness to serve in the dirtiest of ways, but He was also giving us an example to follow. Like Jesus, we must be willing to get our hands dirty. Though we can't wash anyone's heart, we can serve people all around us. If we belong to Jesus, then we will be willing and ready to do so.

Reflect

1. Why was Peter upset with Jesus?

2. What was Jesus trying to show Peter, and us?

3. What are some examples of ways you can serve the people around you today?

Pray

Jesus, thank You that You are the Servant King. Help us to follow Your example and live lives of service to those around us.

One Last Meal

Show

As the family gathers together, ask each person to share their favorite holiday food. They might share things like turkey at Thanksgiving, birthday cake, or ham at Christmas. After each person has a chance to share, remind the family that Jesus was in Jerusalem for the holiday of Passover. At Passover, like the other holidays mentioned, there were special foods the people always ate. But at this Passover, Jesus was going to help His friends see that He was changing the meaning of the meal.

Read

Matthew 26:26–30

Explain

The Passover meal was a meal about remembering. Each piece of the meal helped the people remember they were once slaves in Egypt, and how God had delivered them. But Jesus was changing things. He took the bread and told the disciples that it was His body. He took the cup of wine and told them it was His blood that would be shed for them. Though the disciples didn't know it yet, Jesus was very soon going to be arrested, tried, and put to death on the cross. And through that, God would once again provide deliverance, not from slavery in Egypt, but from slavery to sin.

We still remember this as we celebrate the Lord's Supper. Every time we do, we remember that Jesus gave up His body and His blood for us so we might become the free children of God. Time was growing short for Jesus. Everything had been leading to this.

Reflect

1. What were Jesus and His disciples celebrating?

2. How did Jesus change the meaning of what they were celebrating?

3. How do we still remember the sacrifice of Jesus today?

Pray

Thank You, Jesus, for this great sacrifice. Help us to never forget that You gave Your life for us.

In the Garden

Show

Engage the family in a staring contest. Pair up family members and ask each pair to stare at each other as long as possible until one person blinks. Then have the winners of each pair face off against each other until only one person remains as the staring contest winner. Affirm how difficult it is to keep your eyes open without blinking, but then transition to the next part of the story, telling the family that as Jesus and His disciples finished dinner, they went out to a garden. The disciples had trouble keeping their eyes open, too, even though Jesus asked them to.

Read

Matthew 26:36–46

Explain

Jesus was fully aware of what was about to happen. He knew that He would soon hang on the cross, taking all the sins of mankind on Himself. It would be painful—more pain than any human had ever or would ever experience. And He wanted to ask His Father if there was any other way that God's rescue could be accomplished. He prayed and prayed, asking the Lord if there was another way, but the Father's plan was set. Jesus trusted His Father and submitted to His will for our sake and for God's glory.

The disciples did not know everything that was going to happen. They were tired, and though Jesus asked them to stay awake, they fell asleep again and again. We are very much like the disciples here. We will never really know how much it cost Jesus in order to save us from our sins. We find ourselves sleeping while someone else does the work for us. But this, too, is God's grace for us—that even while we sleep, God is at work on our behalf to deliver us from our sins.

Reflect

1. Why was Jesus so concerned in the garden?

2. What did Jesus pray about there?

3. How are we like the disciples in this part of the story?

Pray

Jesus, thank You that You were willing to submit Yourself fully to the will of the Father. And thank You that even though we do not deserve it, You loved us enough to die for us.

The Traitor

Show

Ask the family if anyone is familiar with the name Benedict Arnold. Briefly explain that Benedict Arnold was a military officer during the Revolutionary War, but then agreed to betray the Americans to the British before he was found out to be a spy. His name has come to mean "traitor," someone who pretends to be a friend but then turns out to be an enemy. Explain that in the next part of the story, you will meet such a traitor.

Read

Matthew 26:47–56

Explain

Jesus was ready. He had His last meal with His friends. He had gained strength from prayer in the garden. And now His time had come. Jesus looked up to see Judas, one of His disciples, approaching, and with him came many others. Judas had agreed in secret to show the religious leaders where Jesus was so they could arrest Him and take Him to the cross. Judas had traveled with Jesus, eaten with Jesus, listened to Jesus teach, and even seen His miracles. But despite all this, Judas never really believed in who Jesus is.

This is a powerful warning to us, letting us know that we, too, might go to church, read the Bible, and sing songs about Jesus. But we must do more—we must believe and ask Jesus to truly forgive us and change our hearts. Being around Jesus is not enough; we must be people of true faith.

Reflect

1. Who was Judas?

2. What was Judas doing in the garden?

3. How does this part of the story serve as a warning for us?

Pray

Jesus, we want to be people of true faith. Help us not to be just people who know things about You, but instead people who truly believe.

Betrayed...Again

Show

Prior to family devotion, gather an index card and pen. Give the index card and pen to the family, and ask them together to think of the name of a famous person from history and secretly write it on the card without letting you see it. Then take the card and put it on your forehead. The goal will be for you to ask questions and try and figure out who you are based on the way the family answers the question. Explain that the purpose of this game was for you to figure out your own identity. As you will see in the next part of the story, Peter was much easier to identify. But Peter was someone who didn't want to be found out.

Read

Matthew 26:69–75

Explain

Everything had gone sideways in the garden. The disciples had no idea what was coming, and when the crowd arrested Jesus, they scattered in fear. Peter had always been the brave one, claiming that he would never walk away from Jesus, but as Jesus was on trial, Peter stood in the shadows. Even though he tried, he couldn't hide. People recognized Peter. But out of fear of what might happen to him, Peter denied that he even knew Jesus not once, not twice, but three times.

Like Judas before him, Peter also denied Jesus. But Peter had a different end to his story than Judas. As soon as Peter came to his senses, he was immediately sorry for what he had done. And in this, we can find great comfort, because there are all kinds of ways in which we might deny Jesus. We might deny Him with the way we act, the words we say, or even the good things we fail to do. Thankfully, Jesus has enough grace to cover all our sins. If we humble ourselves and return to Him, Jesus will receive us back just as He would do for Peter. For now, though, Peter wept as Jesus continued His journey toward the cross.

Reflect

1. What happened to the disciples when Jesus was arrested?

2. How did Peter deny Jesus?

3. Why might this story be of some comfort to us?

Pray

Thank You, Jesus, that Your grace never runs out. Thank You that You stand ready to forgive us for our sins.

At the Cross

Show

When the family is gathered together, hold up two fingers in the shape of a "V." Ask the family if they know what that is a sign for. Likely, someone will recognize it as the symbol for peace. Explain to the family that while most people know that as the symbol for peace, it was once the symbol for "victory." Interestingly, it was a popular symbol during war times. You might say that the symbol was reversed in history. Using that as a building block, introduce the next part of the story, saying that you will read today a very important part of the story—Jesus' death on the cross. Explain that just as this other symbol changed meanings, so also did Jesus' death change the meaning of the cross.

Read

Matthew 27:32–51

Explain

During the days of Jesus, death on the cross was the worst form of punishment imaginable. It was reserved for the worst kinds of criminals because it was so painful and so humiliating. Though Jesus had done nothing wrong, He was hung on a cross between two such criminals to die. Unlike those criminals who were being put to death for their crimes, Jesus was being put to death for the crimes of humanity. He was dying for the sins of people everywhere who would believe in Him. Even in the midst of His pain and suffering, Jesus was able to extend grace to one of these criminals. The door is always open with Jesus for someone to come, believe, and find forgiveness.

When the time had come, Jesus died, and as He did, He accomplished the work God had sent Him to do. When Jesus died, the veil in the temple that separated people from the presence of God was torn in half, from top to bottom, meaning that people now had access to God like never before. Thanks to the death of Jesus, we can approach God unafraid, calling Him Father. Though the cross symbolized death and defeat, Jesus reversed the symbol. The cross, for us, means life and victory.

Reflect

1. What did the cross symbolize?

2. Why was Jesus dying?

3. What does the cross symbolize now?

Pray

Jesus, thank You for dying a death You did not deserve so we could have a life we do not deserve.

He Is Risen

Show

Prior to family devotion, take an egg and poke two small pin holes at each end. Carefully blow into one end of the egg, forcing out the inside and leaving the egg hollow. When the family gathers together, present the egg being careful to not show the family the holes. Ask them what will happen if you crack the egg on the table, then do so, and reveal the empty shell. Transition to the next part of the story by telling the family that they expected to find the egg full when it was opened. Just like that, Jesus' friends expected to find Him in the tomb three days after He died on the cross. But they, too, were in for a surprise.

Read

Luke 24:1–12

Explain

It had been three days of hopelessness, confusion, and despair. The disciples were scattered, and Jesus' friends did not know what to do. Of course they were sad at the death of their friend, but they also had lost hope. They had believed Jesus to be God's rescuer and savior, and they did not understand how He could have died. In their minds, things had gone terribly wrong.

But they had not; everything was happening exactly how God planned it to be. So, when Jesus' friends came to the tomb three days later, they expected to find His body. They did not find Jesus, but instead found two angels who gave them the incredible news. They shouldn't be looking for Jesus where dead people were found, because Jesus was alive!

They could scarcely believe it, but the impossible had happened. Suddenly, they remembered that Jesus told them exactly how it would be. Jesus had risen from the dead, never to die again. Even now, the tomb is still empty; Jesus is still alive and well, and in Him, we too can have eternal life.

Reflect

1. Why did Jesus' friends go to the tomb?

2. What message did they receive?

3. What would you have been thinking if you were among them?

Pray

Jesus, thank You that not even the grave could hold You down. Thank You that You are the risen Lord, alive forevermore.

Burning Hearts

Show

As the family gathers together, ask each person whether or not they like mystery stories. If someone is particularly enthusiastic, ask them to share their favorite mystery story or series. If not, ask the family what some of the things are that make up a good mystery story. Of course, the best thing about a mystery is that even though you might be confused during the story, when you come to the end, all the details throughout the story make sense. Explain that in the next part of the story, the pieces began to fall together for Jesus' friends and followers. They began to see that the whole story, from beginning to end, is really about Jesus.

Read

Luke 24:13–32

Explain

The travelers couldn't believe the stranger they encountered hadn't heard the news. After all, Jesus was what everyone in Jerusalem had been talking about—some even going so far as to say He had risen from the dead. But they did not know they were talking to the man Himself! As they talked together, Jesus did something for these people that He's still doing for people today—that is, He helped them see that the whole story of God, the earth, and humanity is all about Jesus. Jesus is the main character in the story; He's the piece that makes everything else make sense. And when the travelers began to understand this, their hearts burned within them.

The same thing happens to us. We might live our lives thinking that we are the center of the story, but we are not. We are only minor characters in the greatest story ever told—the only real story ever told. We find meaning in life when we come to understand that Jesus does not fit into the story of our lives, but we fit into His.

Reflect

1. What were the travelers talking about?

2. What did Jesus explain to them?

3. Why is it important that we see Jesus as the main character in the story?

Pray

Help us, Lord, not to think too much of ourselves. Help us to see You as the center of the story.

# Week 45 Day 2

The Doubter

Show

As the family gathers together, tell them to get ready, because you are going to take off and fly around the top of the house. Make like you are readying yourself for flight, then ask them whether they believe you or not. Affirm them if they do not, because what you are telling them is obviously impossible. But if you, for example, were able to hover for a few seconds on the chair, they would probably believe. In other words, the family would want proof that you could actually do what you are claiming. Transition to the next part of the story by saying that there were people who couldn't believe Jesus had come back to life. They, too, wanted proof. But unlike the example of you flying, Jesus was able to give them real proof of His resurrection.

Read

John 20:24–29

Explain

It's hard to blame Thomas, isn't it? Jesus had appeared to many people after His resurrection, but to Thomas, the news was too good to be true. He wanted proof before he was ready to believe.

Sometimes faith can feel like that—we want some kind of proof to know the things we are reading in the Bible are true. We should be careful, though, because faith is choosing to believe something that we cannot see; it's believing even though we don't have total proof. But in the case of Thomas, Jesus gave him exactly what he asked for. In His grace, Jesus was willing to meet Thomas in the midst of his doubt and help him believe.

In the same way, we should bring our doubts to Jesus instead of hiding them. In His grace, Jesus can help us believe as well.

Reflect

1. What did Thomas want?

2. How did Jesus help Thomas?

3. What should we do if we are experiencing doubt?

Pray

Jesus, thank You that You show us grace even in our doubts. Help us to trust You enough to bring our doubts to You.

Welcome Back

Show

As the family gathers together, ask them to make a list of all the potential ways they can get into your home. For example, there might be a front door, a back door, a garage code, or even a window. You might have some fun with the example by talking out a scenario of climbing a tree in the backyard to get on the roof and come down the chimney or other scenarios like that. Conclude the discussion by telling the family that all these are ways that you can come home, and it's good that you know all of them. But remind the family that there was still one character in the story that did not know how to come home to Jesus—or if he would even be welcome there. That was Peter.

Read

John 21:15–19

Explain

We saw Peter denying Jesus in the courtyard. We saw him at the empty tomb, struggling to believe. And though he wanted to accept that Jesus was alive, he wasn't sure where that left him. Would he be received back after what he had done? Would he be welcomed home? With these questions, Peter went back to the very thing he was doing before he met Jesus—fishing. But

Jesus is a welcoming Savior; He wanted Peter to come back to Him, and not just come back, but to play an important part in the next section of the story. Instead of angrily lashing out at Peter, Jesus made him breakfast! And He told Peter that he had a job to do. He was to feed the sheep of Jesus; that is, Peter would be a leader in the community of faith, teaching and preaching among them and showing them how to follow Jesus.

How encouraging this is for us, because all of us will fail. We will all sin as we follow Jesus. But like Peter, Jesus will always welcome us back to Him.

Reflect

1. Why was Peter fishing?

2. How did Jesus show Peter he was forgiven?

3. Why is this an encouraging part of the story for us?

Pray

Jesus, thank You that You are rich in grace and mercy. Thank You for reminding us that we can always come home.

Go and Tell

Show

As the family gathers together, ask them to respond to two different commands you are going to give them. The first command is to make their beds. The second command is to change a tire. No doubt the first command is easier to follow because making a bed is probably something everyone in the house has done before. But changing a tire would likely be different. Explain that if you were going to ask them to change the tire, then they would probably need some help. They would likely need you to go with them, to show them how to do it, and to even help them accomplish the task. Explain that in the next part of the story, Jesus is going to give an assignment, not just to His disciples, but to us as well. Explain that this is a very big and difficult assignment, but that Jesus does not just give us the command; He promises us His presence as well.

Read

Matthew 28:18–20

Explain

The disciples didn't exactly know what to expect as they gathered on the hill. They had seen Jesus many times since He rose from the grave, and each time He taught them more and more. But on the hill that day, Jesus was done teaching and was ready to give His friends and followers their marching orders. He was going to tell them their assignment, for He was going back to heaven.

The assignment was simple, but difficult—they were to go to all the world, teaching everyone to believe in Jesus, to be baptized in His name, and to obey Him. These disciples were to make disciples.

This is the same assignment we have today. Regardless of what city we live in, what jobs we have, or how big our families are, we are to be telling people about Jesus and helping them follow Him everywhere we go. Just as it was a big job for the disciples, it's a big job for us. That's why it's such good news that Jesus promises to go with us. He will be with us always, even to the very end of the story.

Reflect

1. What assignment did Jesus give to His followers?

2. How does that assignment apply to us today?

3. Why is it important for us to remember that Jesus is with us always?

Pray

Lord, You have given us important work to do. Help us to make disciples everywhere we go, trusting that You are with us, helping us to accomplish this good work.

All the Nations

Show

As the family gathers together, ask each person to share their favorite sequel. In order to get the conversation going, bring up some examples to the family. You might list *The Empire Strikes Back* as the sequel to *Star Wars*, *Toy Story 2*, or *Frozen 2*. After each person has had a chance to share their favorite sequel, ask them to think a little more deeply about sequels. Specifically, ask them to consider why some movies and books have sequels and some do not. Explain that in order for a sequel to be really good, it must continue the story that was started in the original. Explain that in today's devotion, you will see together the beginning of a "sequel" that continues the story.

Read

Acts 1:1–8

Explain

The book of Luke is one of four books we call the Gospels—Matthew, Mark, Luke, and John. Each of those gospels was written for a different specific purpose, but they all tell the story of Jesus. But Luke is unique among the four because we know the specific person the book was written for. It was for a man named Theophilus who, though he was not a Christian, was nevertheless curious about Jesus and asked Luke to write down the story. But Luke didn't just write the story of Jesus. He wrote the sequel as well.

The sequel to the book of Luke is what we know as the book of Acts. Like the book of Luke, Acts was written to Theophilus to explain what happened next. And what happened next was the beginning of the church. From the very beginning, the church was meant to join God in His mission to share the story of Jesus with the whole world. Though the church would begin in Jerusalem, they were meant to enlarge their circles wider and wider until the whole world knows the story of Jesus. This is the reason any of us heard this story—it's because eventually the story came to us. And we are meant to spread the word wider and wider as well.

Reflect

1. Where were Jesus' followers supposed to share the good news of Jesus?

2. What are some ways you can share the message of Jesus both near and far?

3. How can sharing the gospel with the whole world become more important to our family?

Pray

God in heaven, You love every nation on the earth and want them to hear about Jesus. Please help us care about the world in the same way You do.

Power from Heaven

Show

Before the family gathers together, bring several electrical appliances out and set them before the family. One by one, turn the switches off and on, showing that they do not work. Ask the family what they think is wrong with them, and then point out that none of them are plugged in. In order for the appliance to have power, it must be plugged into the wall outlet—that's the source of the power. Transition to the next section of the story by explaining that Jesus had given the disciples an assignment, but they needed power in order to do so. The power would not come from themselves; instead, the power to be witnesses for Jesus would come from heaven. The disciples were about to be filled with that power.

Read

Acts 2:1–14

Explain

Jesus had told His followers to go to Jerusalem and wait, but they didn't know exactly what they were waiting for. As they were gathered together there, they heard a mighty sound, and they saw something very strange. What looked to be tongues of fire rested above each one of them. The disciples were in the middle of the fulfillment of another of God's promises, one He had made through His prophet Joel. The Holy Spirit was coming upon them in a new way. Just as Joel had prophesied, the Spirit would not come upon a select few and then depart, but instead would dwell within every follower of Jesus.

This is where the power to fulfill Jesus' assignment would come from. Because the Holy Spirit was in them, the disciples were able to be strong witnesses for Jesus. They declared the good news of the death and resurrection of Jesus in languages they did not know, and the people were amazed.

Like the disciples, when we believe in Jesus, the Holy Spirit takes up residence within us. It's important to remember that the Holy Spirit isn't just a power source or some energy; He is God, one with the Father and with Jesus. In giving us the Holy Spirit, God is giving us Himself! This is how Jesus goes with us wherever we go, and this is how we have the power we need to courageously tell others the good news that they can be forgiven and have new life in Christ.

Reflect

1. What happened to the disciples when they were in Jerusalem?

2. When does the Holy Spirit come and live inside a person?

3. Why is it important that we remember the Spirit lives in us if we are believers in Jesus?

Pray

Thank You, God, for giving us the gift of Your Holy Spirit. Help us to keep in step with the Spirit, walking in obedience with how He leads us.

A New Community

Show

To begin family devotion, ask the family how they know if something is alive or not. For example, how do they know that a dog is alive but a rock is not? Explain that in scientific terms, there are seven things that all living things do: they eat, move, breathe, produce waste, react to their surroundings, reproduce, and grow. All living things have these things in common. Explain that the reason you talked about this today is because in yesterday's devotion, you saw that a new community was forming from people who believed the disciples' message. This is the church, and the church is alive. And like all living things, the church started to grow.

Read

Acts 2:40–47

Explain

People did not just hear the message of the disciples; they believed it. And when they did, they were born again to new life in Christ. When someone is born again, they are born with a new heart, new desires, and a new family. That family is the church, and it's made up of people of all different nations, backgrounds, and languages. This is the family of faith—the believing community.

And the very first one started to grow. They ate together, prayed together, learned together from the disciples, and they told more and more people about Jesus.

The church is still alive today, and if we are believers in Jesus, then we are part of this community. The way that we show we are a part of the church is by joining a particular church—a local church. The church is a group of God's people who serve one another in the way God has gifted us, encourage each other to follow Jesus, pray together, and live life together. The church is also to continue preaching the same message of the first disciples with the power of the Holy Spirit, so it will keep growing. The church is God's gift to us to help us follow Jesus, and God's gift to the world to extend the message of the gospel.

Reflect

1. What is the church?

2. What were some of the things the church did in this part of the story?

3. Why is it important that our family is part of a local church?

Pray

Thank You, God, for the gift of the church. Help us to be a family that is faithful to and loves the church.

No Other Name

Show

As the family gathers together, ask them to play a game with you in which they will complete the name of a well-known person. For each of the following, give the person's first name, then ask the family to complete it:

- Abraham . . . Lincoln

- Winston . . . Churchill

- Genghis . . . Khan

Explain that these people from history are so well-known that their last name immediately comes to mind when you hear the first. But further explain that even though those people are well-known, their names don't have any real power anymore. They're just names. Then transition to the next part of the story by saying that when the church began to grow and the gospel spread, it did so because of a single name. And this name is not just well- known; it has power.

Read

Acts 4:1–12

Explain

Peter and John were boldly proclaiming the good news of the gospel. But they weren't only preaching in the name of Jesus; God was also working miracles in the name of Jesus. Not everyone was happy about the spread of this message. The same religious leaders who tried to stop Jesus by putting Him to death arrested Peter and John, warning them that they must keep silent. Though we might not ever be arrested for speaking about Jesus, there always have been and will continue to be people in the world who want that message stopped. But Peter and John knew that this was an impossibility. They had been so changed by Jesus that it would be impossible for them to stop talking about it. Not only that, but they also knew that the name of Jesus had power. It's not that "Jesus" is a magic word; it's that Jesus alone has the power to change the human heart. That's why they could continue to speak His name boldly no matter what the cost might be to them, and that's why we must do the same.

Reflect

1. Why were Peter and John arrested?

2. How did they respond when they were told to stop speaking about Jesus?

3. What can we learn from Peter and John's response?

Pray

Jesus, thank You that there is power in Your name. Help us not be afraid to speak Your name.

Don't Hold Back

Show

As the family gathers together, ask them to play a game called "Two Truths and a Lie." Explain that every family member will need to think of three statements about themselves or what has been happening in their lives. Two of the statements should be true, and one of them should be a lie. Each family member will share their statements and the rest of the family will try and figure out which statement is a lie. Play through the game and see how many lies you can spot. Explain that sometimes it's difficult for us to spot a lie, especially when it sounds like the truth. But then transition to the next part of the story by saying that while such a thing is difficult for us, it's not difficult for God. He knows what's true all the time. This is why we should never try and hold the truth back from God.

Read

Acts 5:1–11

Explain

The early church was marked by their generosity. Whenever someone had a need, someone else would provide for that need, sometimes by selling something that belonged to them and using the money to help. Such was the case with this married couple, Ananias and Saphira—except for the fact that they held back from what they had promised. No one told them to sell their property; no one told them to give the money away. It was their own idea, and it was a good one. But they went wrong by lying about how much money they were going to give. Though they gave the appearance of being generous, their hearts were greedy, and God knew the truth.

The consequences were immediate and severe, and we should take this as a warning—when we follow Jesus, He demands everything we have. This is what it means to call Jesus Lord—it means He is our true Master. He is our Boss. And we should not presume to hold anything back from Him.

Reflect

1. What did Ananias and Saphira do wrong?

2. Why were the consequences so severe?

3. What do we learn from what happened to them?

Pray

You, Jesus, are Lord of all, including us. Forgive us when we try and hold back parts of our lives from You.

A Standing Ovation

Show

Explain to the family that you are going to have a brief family talent show. Ask each person to display a simple talent—turning a cartwheel, telling a joke, kicking a ball—simple, easy actions. After each one, lead the family not only to applaud, but to stand up and applaud. After the show is finished, ask each person what it meant when the family stood to applaud. Affirm that a standing ovation is a high compliment. Transition to the next part of the story by explaining that you will see, in the story, a standing ovation—but you might be surprised who gave it and what it was for.

Read

Acts 7:51–60

Explain

Like Peter and John before him, Stephen was arrested. He was a believer in Jesus, someone who was greatly respected in the church because of the way he served other people. Stephen was falsely accused of speaking badly against God and the Jewish people, and in response, he preached a bold sermon. Stephen was faithful to the truth, even though the truth was difficult for the religious leaders to hear, and in response, they picked up stones and began to throw them at him. Stephen knew he was going to die; in fact, he would be the first of many people who were killed because they believed in Jesus. But before he died, Stephen looked up into the sky and saw Jesus there. But Jesus was not seated at the right hand of God's throne; instead, He was standing up. Perhaps that's because Jesus wanted to acknowledge this man's faithfulness, that Stephen was willing to sacrifice everything for his faith.

Reflect

1. Why was Stephen in trouble?

2. Why do you think Stephen was willing to give up everything rather than abandon his faith?

3. What did he see when he looked into the sky?

Pray

Jesus, we are challenged by the story of your good and faithful servant. Help us to be bold and faithful as we have seen Stephen be.

Scattered

Show

Before the family gathers together, find several medications in the house. Distribute the packages to members of the family, and ask them to read some of the ingredients and the directions for usage, and then point everyone's attention to the warning of potential side effects. Ask the family to discuss what side effects are, then summarize the conversation by telling them that side effects are things that might happen to someone's body other than the intended purpose of the medicine. For example, you don't take medicine to make you dizzy, but the medicine might also cause dizziness in addition to its true purpose. Transition to the next part of the story by reminding the family that yesterday, you read about Stephen's sacrifice for his faith. Today you will read about some unintended side effects of that sacrifice.

Read

Acts 8:1–3

Explain

The religious leaders had killed Jesus. They had arrested Peter and John. Now they had put Stephen to death as well. And that was only the beginning. Persecution—the hurting of people because of their faith—became widespread. All these actions were intended to stop the spread of the message about Jesus. The religious leaders wanted to scare the new church out of talking about Jesus. But their actions did not do what they intended. Rather than stopping the spread of the message, the persecution only forced the new Christians out into other places than Jerusalem. They began preaching and teaching about Jesus further and further out, and more and more people believed. Though this was not what the religious leaders intended, it was precisely what God wanted to happen.

The first steps to completing Jesus' assignment of taking the good news to all the earth had begun. And yet again we see that God is able to take the evil intentions of men and turn them into something good.

Reflect

1. What happened after Stephen's death?

2. How did God use the evil intentions of people for good?

3. Why is that an important thing for us to remember?

Pray

Thank You, God, that You are in control. Help us to remember that You can always take what was meant for evil and bring good from it.

New Believers

Show

Take a piece of bread and display it in front of the family, asking them who is excited to eat this piece of bread. It's likely no one will be too enthusiastic, and explain that's because you have other things in the home to eat. But then ask how their attitude would change if they had not eaten anything for three days—how excited would they be then? The answer, of course, is much more. Transition to the next part of the story by explaining that as the good news of Jesus went out, the message was met with hunger. People were hearing about Jesus for the very first time, and they realized just how much they needed this good news.

Read

Acts 8:4–8

Explain

The Samaritans and the Jews did not get along. Though they believed similar things, they nevertheless did not associate with one another. But now the gospel was going past Jerusalem into Samaria, and it was met with great joy. The Samaritans were believing, and when they were, they were being included in

God's family. God's family is bigger than one group of people; it goes beyond nationality, race, or any other boundary.

This was the first time, though, that a large group of people that were not a part of the Jews had heard this message, and the leaders of the church were going to have to make some choices. Would they accept the fact that the message of Jesus was for all people, or would they try and keep the good news to themselves? Their decision would set the stage for the future, and would be another point at which they would have to decide whether they were going to obey God or not.

Reflect

1. Why was it a big deal that the message of Jesus went to Samaria?

2. What decision would the church leaders have to make?

3. Why is it sometimes hard for us to share the message of Jesus with people who are different than we are?

Pray

Help us to remember, Lord, that the gospel is for all people. Help us not to hold back this good news from anyone.

On the Lookout

Show

Before the family gathers together, take five or six pennies and hide them in easy to find places in the room. Explain to the family that you have hidden these pennies, and then challenge them to find them. When all the pennies are found, explain that one of the reasons they were easily found was that you told them they were hidden. Because you told them the coins were hidden, the family was on the lookout for them. If they didn't know they were there, they might have gone days without finding them all. Explain that in the same way, God has prepared opportunities for us to share the message of Jesus in our daily lives. But if we aren't looking for them, we might pass them by and never notice.

Read

Acts 8:26–35

Explain

God had gone before Philip. He had created the opportunity. And when Philip was obedient to the call of the Spirit, he found a man who was already reading the Scriptures. In fact, all the man needed was someone who could explain to him what he was reading.

Like Philip, God has gone before us in our daily lives. There are opportunities each and every day for us to speak the words of the gospel. The only question is whether or not we will have the faith to actually look for them.

Reflect

1. How do we know God prepared the way for Philip to talk to this man?

2. What was the man reading?

3. How might you be on the lookout for opportunities God has prepared for you to talk about Jesus?

Pray

Lord, thank You for preparing the way for us to have real conversations about You. Help us to be on the lookout for Your work.

Blindness and Sight

Show

Blindfold several members of the family, and then explain that they will have a contest to see who can tie their shoes the quickest. Start the contest and declare a winner. Debrief the contest by asking the family what the most difficult part of it was. Then point back to the story, explaining that you are going to meet someone in the story who suddenly became blind. But he quickly realized that even though he was blind in his eyes for a time, he had been blind in his heart for his whole life.

Read

Acts 9:1–9

Explain

When Stephen was put to death, Saul was there. In fact, Saul was the religious leader who was heading up all of the efforts to do violence against the Christians. Saul thought that the message of Jesus was dangerous, that it was leading people away from the true God of Israel, and he was willing to go to any lengths to stop it.

But God had a different plan for Saul's life. There he was, on his way to another city in which he would once again round up the Christians to do them harm, when he had a personal meeting with Jesus. Saul learned the truth—he was fighting against the very God he thought he was fighting for. He learned that he had been blind his entire life, and though he could not see after meeting Jesus, in another way, he could see the truth for the very first time. Saul, the great hater of Christians, had become one himself.

Reflect

1. Who was Saul?

2. Why did he hate Christians?

3. What happened to him on the road to Damascus?

Pray

God, thank You that Your love and grace know no bounds. Help us to not think of anyone as a lost cause, no matter who they are or what they've done.

Enemy to Ally

Show

Ask the family to play a game of "Password." Pair the family members up. Explain that you will give a secret word to one member of the pair. They will try to get their partner to guess the secret word by only using one-word clues. For example, if the secret word is "dog" then the partner might give the clue of "animal." Continue the game, alternating which person gives a hint, until one pair guesses the secret word. Remind the family that the game was called "Password," and then further explain that people use passwords sometimes to get into special places or meetings. If a person knows the password, it means they are part of the group and can be let in. Now point back the story, reminding the family that before Saul met Jesus, he was the leader of the persecution against Christians. But then he became a Christian. The question, as we will see, was whether the community of faith would trust him enough to let him come in.

Read

Acts 9:26–30

Explain

The early church did not know quite what to do with Saul. They had spent months fearing him, avoiding him, and being careful of him because he was leading the persecution against them. But now here he was, claiming he had some miraculous encounter with Jesus, and saying that he was a Christian. What to do? Was it a trick to get inside their ranks? Would he turn on them if they trusted him? It was a big choice about whether to believe him. But one among them, a man named Barnabas, was willing to take that risk. He stood up for Saul, and he persuaded others that his turning to Jesus was indeed real.

Barnabas was willing to take a chance on Saul, and he was right to do so. In fact, Saul—or Paul, as we know him today—is one of the main characters of the next part of the story. One of the ways we show, as Christians, that Jesus is real in our lives is through the way we treat other people. Like Barnabas, we should be willing, as much as we are able, to accept anyone who believes in Jesus. Our doors, and our hearts, should be open to those who come into faith.

Reflect

1. Why was the church nervous about Saul?

2. How did Barnabas help?

3. Why should we be open, as Christians, to new people coming into the church?

Pray

Help us, Lord, to have open hearts. Help us to warmly embrace those who begin new relationships with Jesus.

No Favorites

Show

Present a stack of several small candies before the family. Distribute them to the family members, but do so unevenly. Base the distribution on some arbitrary characteristics—people with glasses get double, those wearing the color blue get more than other colors, etc. Explain to the family why the distribution was uneven, and then ask them if they think it was fair. Of course it is not. Redistribute the candies evenly, then explain that if you had left the distribution as it was, you would be showing favoritism to some members of the family over others. Then bring the family back to the story by telling them that you will see today, again, that God does not show favoritism to one group of people over another.

Read

Acts 10:30–36

Explain

The gospel had begun to spread. The message of the death and resurrection of Jesus moved beyond Jerusalem and into Samaria, but it did not stop there. The gospel is meant to go to the entire world. Unfortunately, though, there were still those among the Jewish believers who had trouble accepting that all the rest of the world was welcome in the family of God.

One man named Cornelius worshiped the true God, but he was not a Jew. So, God stepped in to make it clear that he, and anyone else who had faith in Jesus, was welcome in His family. God gave Cornelius and Peter dreams at the same time which showed them clearly that Peter was to go and share the message of God's grace with Cornelius and his family. Peter was obedient, and Cornelius's family believed and were saved from their sin. As Peter saw, God does not show favoritism, and neither should we. All people are sinners regardless of their background, and all people are welcome in God's family when they believe in Jesus.

Reflect

1. Who was Cornelius?

2. How did God show Peter that Cornelius and his family were welcome in God's family?

3. What implications does this story have for us today?

Pray

Thank You, Lord, that You are a welcoming Father. Help us also to welcome people regardless of where they come from or what may be different about them than us.

Christians

Show

Ask the family to share some of their favorite nicknames. They might be nicknames they themselves have, nicknames of their friends, or nicknames of famous people, like athletes. Then ask the family to discuss how someone gets a certain nickname. Affirm that a nickname can come in all different kinds of ways, but then transition to the next part of the story, telling the family that the word *Christian* is actually a nickname. And you will see today where it came from.

Read

Acts 11:19–26

Explain

The gospel marched on. After Stephen was killed and the persecution against the church broke out, some of the believers in Jesus went all the way to a city called Antioch. These believers were faithful to share the good news of Jesus, and many people believed in that city. So many believed, in fact, that the church in Jerusalem sent Barnabas to see what was happening.

Barnabas, as he had done with Saul, was glad to see these new believers. He encouraged them in their faith, and he did not doubt that their faith was real. But these new believers needed to know more about how to follow Jesus, and so Barnabas found Saul and brought him there as well. Together, the two taught this new group of believers, and they learned together to follow Jesus. In fact, they followed Jesus so closely they earned the nickname "Christians," which means "little Christs." Though the people who gave them this nickname might have meant it as an insult, it was a badge of honor. These people knew that to be a Christian meant shaping your life to look like that of Jesus. Today, if we call ourselves Christians, it means the same thing. It means we are, in every way, seeking to make our lives look like that of Christ.

Reflect

1. How did the gospel come to Antioch?

2. What did Barnabas find there, and what did he do?

3. What does it mean to be called a "Christian"?

Pray

It is an honor, Jesus, to bear Your name. Help our lives so closely to resemble Yours that we can rightly be called Christians.

True Escape

Show

Prior to family devotion, gather together two pieces of rope or cloth long enough to tie legs of the family members together. Ask for three volunteers, and stand them in a line. Bind the legs of the person in the middle to one of the legs of the people on each side of them, then give the trio a task to do, like go into the other room and make the bed. After they perform the task, ask them what was hard about doing so while being tied together. Then transition to the next part of the story, saying that you will read today about when Peter was bound to two other people in prison. But as you will see, even being chained to guards was no match for God's ability to rescue.

Read

Acts 12:1–11

Explain

As the gospel continued to spread, so did opposition to it. In fact, the opposition to the gospel had become so fierce that one of the rulers at the time, Herod, actually put James the brother of John to death. Peter, meanwhile, was arrested for continuing to speak about Jesus and put under heavy guard with two soldiers chained to him. All the while, the church continued to pray for

Peter, and God answered their prayers. Even though Peter was firmly secured and guarded, God sent His angel to rescue Peter.

But what about James? While Peter escaped, James did not. Or at least he did not escape in the same way Peter did. Jesus had already provided the greatest rescue for all of us, including James. So while James might have lost his life, he gained eternal life in Christ because he believed in Jesus.

God always provides a rescue for His people. Sometimes that rescue comes in miraculous ways, and sometimes it does not. But if we believe in Jesus, we can know for sure that God will deliver us from the chains of sin and death, even if He chooses not to deliver us in this life.

Reflect

1. Why were James and Peter arrested?

2. How did God provide a rescue for each of them?

3. Why is it important for us to remember that Jesus has already rescued us from sin and death?

Pray

Thank You, Lord, that You are our Rescuer. When we pray and ask You for deliverance, help us to trust in Your wisdom to provide the right deliverance at the right time.

Sent Out

Show

Bring a suitcase with you to family devotion. After the family gathers together, ask the family to imagine that you are going to go together on a trip to a place to tell people about Jesus. Explain that they each have one minute to get one thing they think the family would need on this mission and bring it back to the suitcase. After the minute has passed, ask each family member what they chose to put in the suitcase and allow them to explain why. Then explain that in the next part of the story, you are going to see the first mission trip begin, and it will involve some people you have met before.

Read

Acts 13:1–3

Explain

While people had traveled and shared the gospel before, this was the first moment when a church had set apart specific people to send them out on mission. This also marks an important point in Paul's life, because after this, he would spend the rest of his life going to new places to share the gospel with people who have never heard it before. But Paul and Barnabas had something even more important than a suitcase for their journey; they had the calling of God and the support of the church.

While God tells all of us to share the message of Jesus everywhere we go, He calls out certain people to go farther out and share the message with people who have never had a chance to hear it. Because God is calling these people, the church must be ready to support them as they go with things like prayer, money, and other resources. We must be willing both to be one of the people who will go, and one of the people who will support those who go.

Reflect

1. In your own words, what happened to Paul and Barnabas in this part of the story?

2. Why is it important that they were sent out from the church?

3. How can our family both be ready to go, and also support others who are going?

Pray

Lord, You are still calling people to go to the ends of the earth. Help us to be open to Your call, and to be generous when we see others being called.

Faith Alone

Show

Explain to the family that you are going to have a push-up contest. Ask for two or three volunteers, and then have them assume the push-up position. But for the strongest volunteer, make them do their push-ups with books balanced on their back. Obviously, the strongest person will not be able to do their push-ups as well as the others. Explain that it was an unfair contest because you put extra weight on one person's back. Use the illustration to move into the next part of the story, explaining that the church had come to a decision point. As new people were becoming Christians, they had to decide what those people who were becoming Christians had to do. In other words, they had to decide if they were going to put extra weight on them or not.

Read

Acts 15:1–12

Explain

The gospel message continued to go out. People like Paul and Barnabas had been out in the wider world, and they had seen many people from many different countries believe in Jesus. But the church back in Jerusalem was not so sure yet. They knew that the message of Jesus had started with the Jewish people, but now other people who were not Jews—like Cornelius—were believing also. They had to decide whether or not these new people were really Christians, or whether these people had to become Jews before becoming Christians. If they had to become Jews, it meant they would have to do things like stop eating certain foods, observe certain holidays, and other things. In the end, the church decided, with the guidance of the Holy Spirit, they should not weigh down these new believers. They knew the only thing it took to become a Christian was faith in Jesus.

We must remember this today as well, so we don't put more weight on people as they come to faith. Faith alone in Christ alone—this is the way of salvation.

Reflect

1. Why did the church in Jerusalem have to make a decision?

2. What did they decide?

3. Why does this matter for us today?

Pray

Thank You, God, that it is only by faith and faith alone that we come to Jesus. Help us to remember that as we share the good news of Jesus with others.

Learning by Doing

Show

Prior to family devotion, find a manual for some item in your home. For example, find an owner's manual for the refrigerator, a car, or some other appliance, and bring it with you. Ask a family member to use the manual to fix a problem with that appliance. For example, if you have brought the owner's manual for a vehicle, say that the car is making a funny noise when you start it, and hand them the owner's manual. Then lead a discussion about the difference between having a manual, and having someone with you to show you how to deal with a problem. For complicated issues, it's far better to learn from someone else rather than just having a book to explain it to you. Explain that helping people grow in their faith happens in the same way. This is one of the reasons why Paul often traveled with other people, so they could learn what he was doing and then do the same thing.

Read

Acts 16:1–5

Explain

Timothy was very different than Paul. They had different backgrounds, different perspectives, and different upbringings. But Paul thought of Timothy, a much younger man, as his son in the faith. Paul had helped Timothy grow in his faith, and he was now bringing Timothy along with him so he could learn how to help others.

This is how things are meant to work in God's family. We are to help each other grow up in our faith, but as we are doing so, we are also helping other people get ready to help other people grow. In this way, faith in Jesus multiplies. It's important we understand this—you are never too young or too old to help someone grow in their faith, just as Paul did with Timothy. If we keep reading the Bible, we find that Paul later wrote Timothy some letters because Timothy became a pastor. He took what he learned from Paul and put it into practice.

Reflect

1. Who was Timothy?

2. Why might Paul have brought Timothy with him on his journeys?

3. Who is one person you might be able to help grow in their faith?

Pray

God, thank You for putting people in our lives who can help us grow as we follow You. Help us to play that same role for someone else.

Singing in an Earthquake

Show

As the family gathers together, tell them you'd like to review with them what to do in the case of a natural disaster. Ask the family if they know what to do in the case of a hurricane, then explain that in a hurricane, you would try and cover all the windows with protection and move away from the coast. Ask them what to do in the case of a tornado, then explain that in a tornado, you would want to go to a room below ground, like a basement, if possible. Then ask them what to do in the case of an earthquake, and explain that in an earthquake you would want to stand in a doorway, away from things that might fall and hurt you. Then transition to the next part of the story, telling the family that Paul, too, experienced an earthquake. But this earthquake was unique because it was meant just for him and his friend, Silas.

Read

Acts 16:25–34

Explain

Paul and his ministry companion, Silas, had been thrown in jail. They were put there because they commanded a demon that was inside a woman to come out. Problem is, the woman was a slave, and her master was making money off of her because the demon was predicting the future for people. With the demon gone, so was the master's source of income, so he had the two men thrown in prison. Now Paul and Silas might have done many things in jail. They might have begged for their release; they might have felt sorry for themselves; they might have been angry at being treated unfairly. But instead, the two men spent their time singing praises to God.

This is a powerful lesson for us, that when things go badly in life, we can either choose to get angry or we can choose to believe that God is still in control and worship Him instead. God, meanwhile, had a plan for the two men, and caused an earthquake that broke them free. But rather than escaping, Paul and Silas chose to stay and share the good news of Jesus with the very jailer who was holding them prisoner. Paul and Silas show us not only how to respond to hard times, but they also show us that our hard times can be an opportunity to share the gospel with others.

Reflect

1. Why were Paul and Silas in prison?

2. How did they respond to being in prison?

3. Why is it important for us to remember what Paul and Silas did after the earthquake?

Pray

Lord, the message of Jesus is the most important thing in the world. Help us to remember just how important it is, even in challenging times.

The Message in Athens

Show

Ask the family if anyone remembers the old story of Hansel and Gretel. Ask for a volunteer to briefly tell the story, or read it together if no one can recall it. Then in review, ask them why the two children left the breadcrumbs on the ground. Explain that the breadcrumbs were meant to be a trail to follow. Then explain that in a similar way, God has left breadcrumbs throughout the world. These are little clues about the truth of the universe, who He is, and the message of Jesus. One of the ways we share the gospel with other people is by helping those people see the breadcrumbs that are already in their paths. This is what Paul did when he preached the message of Jesus in Athens.

Read

Acts 17:16–23

Explain

Athens was a well-regarded city, the center of education and learning. In fact people went to the middle of the city every day just to hear other people talk about different philosophies and things they had learned. Paul went there too because he wanted to share the message of Jesus wherever he went. But instead of starting his message with the truth that God created all things, he started with something the people would have been familiar with. There were statues to all kinds of gods in the city, including one statue that was meant to honor an unknown god. Paul used this as a way to introduce the message of the gospel to the people there.

When we share the message of Jesus with other people, one of the things we should do is try and find how God might have prepared the way for this message. It might be that we are able to talk with someone about what's happening in their lives, something they have read, or some other part of their background. When we do that, we help people connect with and understand the message of Jesus in an easier way.

Reflect

1. How did Paul begin his message to the people of Athens?

2. What can we learn from that about sharing the gospel with others?

3. Who is one person you would like to share the message of Jesus with?

Pray

Thank You, Lord, that You are at work all around us. Help us to be on the lookout for all the ways You have prepared the way for us to speak the truth about Jesus.

The Eloquent Preacher

Show

Prior to the family gathering together, put different kinds of food in four or five different bowls. Be sure, though, that the food is hidden in the bowls under a napkin or towel so the family can't see what it is. Then ask for a volunteer, blindfold them, and ask them to identify each of the foods in the bowls using only their touch. When they've tried to identify all of them, take off the blindfold. Explain that an exercise like this is difficult when you can't use all your senses. It would obviously be much easier if you were able to use more than one sense, and even easier if you could use all your senses. Then explain that in the Bible, the church is sometimes referred to as a body. One of the reasons the Bible refers to the church like this is to emphasize that every part of the church is valuable. In today's part of the story, you will meet another part of the body that needed help from the rest of the body.

Read

Acts 18:24–28

Explain

Apollos was a great preacher—even better, probably, than Paul. People loved to listen to Apollos talk about the Scriptures, just as we enjoy hearing great teachers and preachers today. Unfortunately, Apollos had some things to learn. While he was great at giving a message, he didn't know all he needed to about Jesus and especially the Holy Spirit. Thankfully, there were some other believers who were willing to help Apollos learn.

We can learn a great deal from this married couple, Priscilla and Aquilla. Though they might not have had the same gift as Apollos, they were able to use their own gifts to help him grow just as we should be willing to use our gifts to help people in the church grow. At the same time, we can learn a great deal from Apollos. He could have been so proud of his own gift that he was not willing to accept help and correction from other people. But not only was Apollos gifted; he was also humble enough to accept help. We should be the same way, knowing that we are an important part of the body, but also knowing that other parts of the body can help us.

Reflect

1. Who was Apollos?

2. How did Priscilla and Aquilla help Apollos?

3. What are some of the things we should learn from all three?

Pray

Thank You, Lord, for the gift of the church. Please help us to use our gifts to help others grow, and help us to be humble enough to receive help from others.

The Gospel Flourishes

Show

Bring a set of dominoes with you to family devotion. Challenge the family to create a domino chain, one in which you can tap the domino on the end, and all of them fall in sequence. Allow some time for the family to complete the challenge, and then transition back to the story by explaining that like these dominoes, we are seeing the gospel spread to all parts of the world. Like a chain reaction, the gospel is shared, people believe, and then it is shared all the more. And Paul continued to lead the charge. But as you will see in today's part of the story, the spreading of the gospel also caused other dominoes to fall.

Read

Acts 19:11–19

Explain

Not only was Paul preaching, but the Lord was performing all kinds of miracles through him. These miracles only served to make people believe even more in the message about Jesus that Paul shared. There were even those who tried to take advantage of the message of Jesus, claiming they too were messengers of the good news. But in the city of Ephesus, when people who didn't really believe in Jesus tried to work miracles in His name, things did not go well for them.

Meanwhile, more and more people believed in the message, and as a result, they started getting rid of all the idols to other gods they had. But that caused another domino to fall. In Ephesus, people made lots of money by creating idols, and they were not happy with people who threw them away and stopped making them. The gospel is bad for the idol business! Paul would soon find himself in the middle of an angry city. But even this was yet another opportunity for Paul to share the gospel, and the gospel message continued to grow and flourish.

Reflect

1. What was happening in the city of Ephesus?

2. Why were people mad at Paul?

3. How did Paul treat the fact that people were angry at him?

Pray

Thank You, Lord, that the gospel continues to flourish even today. Please help us to be faithful to the message of Jesus even if it has consequences.

Predicting Prison

Show

When the family has gathered together, pull out a phone and look for the daily weather forecast. Share the forecast with the family, and then ask them how they might respond if they have information about the daily weather. They might, for example, change what they were going to wear, make sure to bring an umbrella, or even change plans if the weather is going to be bad. Explain that having an idea of what is going to happen in the future can make us change our behavior in the present. Then explain that next in the story, Paul got not just an idea, but a prediction of what would happen in his future. But knowing what would happen did not make him change what he was doing.

Read

Acts 21:1–14

Explain

After Paul started following Jesus, his life had one purpose: to share the good news about Jesus everywhere he could. That mission had taken him to many parts of the world on missionary journeys. It had also put him in some difficult situations. In his life, Paul would experience all kinds of anger, beatings, troubles, and even things like shipwrecks, all because he continued to speak about Jesus wherever he went.

In this case, Paul received a message from a prophet that if he continued on his way to Jerusalem, he would be bound as a prisoner. Though many of his friends thought this news should make him change course, Paul knew better. He knew that his mission remained to share the gospel everywhere he went, even if that meant sharing the gospel as a prisoner. So Paul continued on his way, not because he wanted to be put in prison, but because he trusted in Jesus and knew that he must follow Him wherever He was leading.

Reflect

1. What message did Paul receive?

2. How might that message have changed Paul's plans for the future?

3. What does Paul's reaction show us about how he felt about the message of Jesus?

Pray

Lord, the gospel is the most important message in the universe. Please help us to treat this good news like the most important news.

The Prisoner Appeals

Show

Bring a pair of glasses or sunglasses with you to family devotion. Ask each member of the family to try them on, look around, and describe how their vision changes when they put them on. Then explain that a pair of glasses changes the way a person looks at the world. Further explain that when we become Christians, it's like we put on a new pair of glasses, and the way we view the world is changed. Point out that you have seen this happen in the life of Paul, and for Paul, he now saw everything as a chance to spread the good news of Jesus.

Read

Acts 25:1–12

Explain

The prediction had come true. Paul was imprisoned because of his faith and preaching about Jesus. But even in his imprisonment, Paul continued to share the gospel message. He was imprisoned not just for a few days, but for months that grew into years as he went from trial to trial.

Paul was a Roman citizen, and one of the rights that any Roman citizen had was to ask for their case to be heard by Caesar, the ruler of the Roman Empire. Eventually, that's exactly what Paul did. But Paul made this appeal not just because he hoped to be released, but more because he wanted the chance to travel to Rome and speak the message of Jesus there. He knew that by making this appeal he would eventually be able to speak before more and more people, and more and more people could hear the good news of the gospel.

Reflect

1. What did Paul have the right to do as a Roman citizen?

2. Why did Paul make this appeal?

3. What do we learn about the importance of the gospel from Paul?

Pray

Lord, help us to view the world through the lens of the gospel. Help us to see every situation we are in as a chance to spread the good news about Jesus.

Rome at Last

Show

Ask the family to imagine that each one of them has been given the opportunity to deliver a speech in front of a group of world leaders, but they only have five minutes to do so. Each person needs to decide what one topic their speech will cover. Give some time to think, then ask each family member to respond with their topic and explain why they chose that one. Conclude the discussion by explaining that with an opportunity like this, you would not want to waste it; you would want to think carefully about the most important thing you could say. Then transition to the next part of the story by explaining that as you will see today, Paul actually had an opportunity like this.

Read

Acts 28:11–22

Explain

Paul had appealed to Caesar, but the road to Rome was a long one. He had traveled for months and endured hardship after hardship, but finally, he reached Rome as a prisoner. Paul did not see his imprisonment as a hindrance, but instead as an opportunity. He would have the opportunity to speak about Jesus in Rome, the most important city in the world at that time, and some of the most powerful and important people in the world would hear this message. Even though Paul was a prisoner, he saw his hardship as an opportunity to continue to speak the good news about Jesus.

The same thing can be true of us. We will walk through discouraging, sad, and dark days. But many times, days like that are a chance for us to speak about our hope in Jesus, and to explain that everyone everywhere can have that same hope.

Reflect

1. Why did Paul not see his imprisonment as a hardship?

2. What did Paul have to believe about the gospel and Jesus in order for him to have this view?

3. Are you having a difficult time right now? How might this present an opportunity for you to share the good news of Jesus with others?

Pray

Thank You, Lord, for this example of how important the message of the gospel is. Help us, also, to know the importance of this message so we will freely share it with others.

Without Hindrance

Show

Walk the family to the kitchen sink and turn on the faucet just enough for it to drip. Then ask the family to consider: Would anything happen if we just let this faucet keep dripping? What if it dripped like this for a year? For ten years? For a hundred years? Use this illustration to explain that even though something small might not seem like much, given enough time and enough consistency, great power can come from it. Then transition to the story by explaining that Paul consistently shared the gospel wherever he went. And we are today still feeling the effects of that.

Read

Acts 28:30–31

Explain

We don't actually know how Paul's life ended. What happened after those two years? Many think Paul was eventually executed for his faith in Jesus, but we just don't know. But while we don't know the specifics of how his life ended, we do know that he continued to share about the Lord Jesus Christ until the very end. Paul ended his life doing the same thing he had done since he was blinded on the road to Damascus: inviting anyone and everyone to repent of their sins and put their faith in Jesus.

It might seem like we aren't making much of a difference in the world when we have simple conversations about Jesus with others. But we should remember that the same action performed over a long period of time has tremendous impact. We should live in such a way that the message of Jesus is without hindrance in us.

Reflect

1. What did Paul spend his life doing?

2. How did Paul's life end?

3. What can we learn from the way Paul spent his life?

Pray

Thank You, Lord, for entrusting us with the same message you entrusted to Paul. Help us to be faithful messengers throughout our whole lives.

Coming Soon

Show

As the family gathers together, ask them what kinds of things you would need to do as a family if you knew that a blizzard was going to hit your town. You might, for example, make sure you had plenty of bottled water and food. You might check your pipes and heater. You might even make sure there was firewood stacked nearby. You would make all these preparations because you knew what was coming. Explain that you are going to begin reading the very end of the story today, things that are going to happen but have not happened yet as described in the book of Revelation. And just as the family would need to be ready for a blizzard, you should also be ready for the end of the story when Jesus comes back.

Read

Revelation 1:1–8

Explain

Jesus is coming back. He said this to John, who wrote down the vision God gave him in the book of Revelation. But when Jesus comes back, it will not be in the same way He came the first time. The first time Jesus came to earth, He was easily mistaken for someone else. He was born in poverty, the son of a common father. Many people never understood His true identity. But when He comes again, no more mistakes will be made. Everyone will know with absolute clarity that Jesus is the King of the Universe.

This will be the best of news for some, and the worst of news for others, because when Jesus comes back, it will be too late to repent and believe in Him. All those who have trusted in Jesus and been rescued from their sin by Him will be able to rejoice, because everything they have believed in will become reality. But for those who have not trusted in Jesus, it will be too late. This is all the more reason for us to trust in Jesus today, because we do not know when He will return.

Reflect

1. How will the return of Jesus be different than when He came the first time?

2. Why will His return be both good and bad news?

3. Why should we not delay in trusting in Jesus to rescue us from our sin?

Pray

Jesus, You are coming back, and You are coming soon. Help us to live in light of the fact that You could return at any moment.

Rescued to Worship

Show

When the family is gathered together, explain that you are going to have a contest to see which member of the family can name the most nations on the earth. Sit or stand in a circle, and go around the circle with each family member naming a nation on earth. Continue around the circle with each person naming a nation without duplicating any that have already been said. If a family member isn't able to think of another nation, then they're out of the game. Continue the process until only one family member remains. Then tell the family that you are coming very close to the end of the story, and you are seeing not things that have already happened, but things that will happen. And as the story continues, you will see what's to become of everyone who trusts in Jesus to rescue them.

Read

Revelation 7:9–12

Explain

Way back in the days of Abraham, God called His people to be a blessing to the nations of the earth. Then Jesus told us that we should share the gospel with every nation on earth. Then in the days of Paul the gospel began to spread to every nation on earth. And someday, there will be people from every nation, from every language, from every part of the world who have all been rescued from their sin by Jesus. This is the family of God, the people He has been building since the very beginning of the story.

Someday, we will all be together and we will worship Jesus because of who He is and what He has done. In the meantime, though, we should look forward to this moment. One of the ways we look forward to this is by making sure we continue to share about the good news of Jesus and invite more and more people into the kingdom of God.

Reflect

1. Who, in this part of the story, is around the throne?

2. What are they doing?

3. How does a person get to be among those who will someday worship Jesus around His throne?

Pray

Jesus, the whole story is moving toward this moment, when we will gather together to worship You. Help us to look forward to this with even more excitement.

All Things New

Show

Bring a children's puzzle with you to family devotion today. As the family gathers together, spread out the pieces before them, and encourage them to begin working to put it together. As they are doing so, explain that this whole story has been a bit like a puzzle. You remember at the beginning, God created everything, and it was flawless. But when sin came into the world, everything was broken apart, like this puzzle. But since then, God has been on a mission to put everything back together again. He has been bringing people back to know Him and love Him, changing their hearts and making them whole again. And today, you will read the end of that story.

Read

Revelation 21:1–5

Explain

Just imagine it. Imagine a time and a place when there is no more crying, no more pain, no more death. This is what God is putting back together for us. But the best part of it all is that in that time, and in that place, we will fully know God. He will at long last be fully with us, and we will be fully with Him. This is the new heaven and earth that ends the story, and we will live there with God and each other for all time.

Because we know this is true about our future, we can live with great hope and joy in the present. We can know that God is going to finish His story, and the ending is the happiest one we could imagine.

Reflect

1. What sticks out to you the most about this description of what's to come?

2. Why is it important for us to remember how the story ends?

3. How might remembering the ending of the story help you in life right now?

Pray

Thank You, God, that You are going to finish this story. Help us to live with hope and joy because we know where You are taking us.

also available from

MICHAEL KELLEY

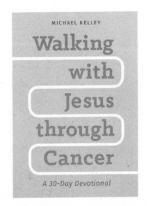

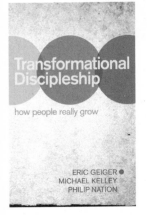

PUBLISHING